D0848586

OPPOSING
VIEWPOINTS®
SERIES

The Legalization
of Marijuana

Other Books of Related Interest:

Opposing Viewpoints Series

America's Prisons

Gun Violence

Police Brutality

Tobacco and Smoking

At Issue Series

Club Drugs

Guns and Crime

Mexico's Drug War

Teen Smoking

Current Controversies Series

Drug Legalization

Gangs

Medical Ethics

Prescription Drugs

"Congress shall make
no law . . . abridging
the freedom of speech,
or of the press."

First Amendment to the US Constitution

The basic foundation of our democracy is the First Amendment guarantee of freedom of expression. The Opposing Viewpoints series is dedicated to the concept of this basic freedom and the idea that it is more important to practice it than to enshrine it.

OPPOSING VIEWPOINTS® SERIES

The Legalization of Marijuana

Noël Merino, Book Editor

GREENHAVEN PRESS
A part of Gale, Cengage Learning

GALE
CENGAGE Learning·

Farmington Hills, Mich • San Francisco • New York • Waterville, Maine
Meriden, Conn • Mason, Ohio • Chicago

Judy Galens, *Manager, Frontlist Acquisitions*

© 2016 Greenhaven Press, a part of Gale, Cengage Learning.

Gale and Greenhaven Press are registered trademarks used herein under license.

For more information, contact:
Greenhaven Press
27500 Drake Rd.
Farmington Hills, MI 48331-3535
Or you can visit our Internet site at gale.cengage.com

ALL RIGHTS RESERVED.
No part of this work covered by the copyright herein may be reproduced, transmitted, stored, or used in any form or by any means graphic, electronic, or mechanical, including but not limited to photocopying, recording, scanning, digitizing, taping, Web distribution, information networks, or information storage and retrieval systems, except as permitted under Section 107 or 108 of the 1976 United States Copyright Act, without the prior written permission of the publisher.

For product information and technology assistance, contact us at

Gale Customer Support, 1-800-877-4253
For permission to use material from this text or product, submit all requests online at www.cengage.com/permissions

Further permissions questions can be emailed to permissionrequest@cengage.com

Articles in Greenhaven Press anthologies are often edited for length to meet page requirements. In addition, original titles of these works are changed to clearly present the main thesis and to explicitly indicate the author's opinion. Every effort is made to ensure that Greenhaven Press accurately reflects the original intent of the authors. Every effort has been made to trace the owners of copyrighted material.

Cover Image copyright © Iriana Shiyan/Shutterstock.com.

LIBRARY OF CONGRESS CATALOGING-IN-PUBLICATION DATA

The legalization of marijuana / Noël Merino, Book Editor.
      pages cm. -- (Opposing viewpoints)
   Includes bibliographical references and index.
   ISBN 978-0-7377-7556-3 (hardcover) -- ISBN 978-0-7377-7557-0 (pbk.)
   1. Marijuana--Law and legislation--United States. 2. Drug legalization--United
States. I. Merino, Noël, editor.
   KF3891.M2L43 2016
   364.1'77--dc23
                                     2015030378

Printed in Mexico
1 2 3 4 5 6 7 20 19 18 17 16

Contents

Chapter 3: Should Use of Medical Marijuana Be Legal?

Chapter 4: Should Recreational Use of Marijuana Be Legal?

Why Consider Opposing Viewpoints?

> "The only way in which a human being can make some approach to knowing the whole of a subject is by hearing what can be said about it by persons of every variety of opinion and studying all modes in which it can be looked at by every character of mind. No wise man ever acquired his wisdom in any mode but this."
>
> John Stuart Mill

In our media-intensive culture it is not difficult to find differing opinions. Thousands of newspapers and magazines and dozens of radio and television talk shows resound with differing points of view. The difficulty lies in deciding which opinion to agree with and which "experts" seem the most credible. The more inundated we become with differing opinions and claims, the more essential it is to hone critical reading and thinking skills to evaluate these ideas. Opposing Viewpoints books address this problem directly by presenting stimulating debates that can be used to enhance and teach these skills. The varied opinions contained in each book examine many different aspects of a single issue. While examining these conveniently edited opposing views, readers can develop critical thinking skills such as the ability to compare and contrast authors' credibility, facts, argumentation styles, use of persuasive techniques, and other stylistic tools. In short, the Opposing Viewpoints Series is an ideal way to attain the higher-level thinking and reading skills so essential in a culture of diverse and contradictory opinions.

In addition to providing a tool for critical thinking, Opposing Viewpoints books challenge readers to question their own strongly held opinions and assumptions. Most people form their opinions on the basis of upbringing, peer pressure, and personal, cultural, or professional bias. By reading carefully balanced opposing views, readers must directly confront new ideas as well as the opinions of those with whom they disagree. This is not to argue simplistically that everyone who reads opposing views will—or should—change his or her opinion. Instead, the series enhances readers' understanding of their own views by encouraging confrontation with opposing ideas. Careful examination of others' views can lead to the readers' understanding of the logical inconsistencies in their own opinions, perspective on why they hold an opinion, and the consideration of the possibility that their opinion requires further evaluation.

Evaluating Other Opinions

To ensure that this type of examination occurs, Opposing Viewpoints books present all types of opinions. Prominent spokespeople on different sides of each issue as well as well-known professionals from many disciplines challenge the reader. An additional goal of the series is to provide a forum for other, less known, or even unpopular viewpoints. The opinion of an ordinary person who has had to make the decision to cut off life support from a terminally ill relative, for example, may be just as valuable and provide just as much insight as a medical ethicist's professional opinion. The editors have two additional purposes in including these less known views. One, the editors encourage readers to respect others' opinions—even when not enhanced by professional credibility. It is only by reading or listening to and objectively evaluating others' ideas that one can determine whether they are worthy of consideration. Two, the inclusion of such viewpoints encourages the important critical thinking skill of objectively evaluating an author's credentials and bias. This evaluation will illuminate an author's reasons for taking a particular stance on an issue and will aid in readers' evaluation of the author's ideas.

It is our hope that these books will give readers a deeper understanding of the issues debated and an appreciation of the complexity of even seemingly simple issues when good and honest people disagree. This awareness is particularly important in a democratic society such as ours in which people enter into public debate to determine the common good. Those with whom one disagrees should not be regarded as enemies but rather as people whose views deserve careful examination and may shed light on one's own.

Thomas Jefferson once said that "difference of opinion leads to inquiry, and inquiry to truth." Jefferson, a broadly educated man, argued that "if a nation expects to be ignorant and free . . . it expects what never was and never will be." As individuals and as a nation, it is imperative that we consider the opinions of others and examine them with skill and discernment. The Opposing Viewpoints series is intended to help readers achieve this goal.

David L. Bender and Bruno Leone,
Founders

Introduction

"Over less than a decade, public opinion has shifted dramatically toward support for the legalization of marijuana."

—William A. Galston and E.J. Dionne Jr., "The New Politics of Marijuana Legalization: Why Opinion Is Changing," Brookings Institution, May 29, 2013

When Gallup, the research organization, began polling Americans in 1969 about whether or not marijuana use should be legal, only 12 percent of Americans said that it should be legal. Yet, by 2015 a Pew Research Center survey found that 53 percent of Americans believe the use of marijuana should be made legal. Not surprisingly, given the shift in opinion, more than one in three of those who said marijuana should be legal had undergone a change of opinion on the issue. Despite the majority support for marijuana legalization, it is not a huge majority and public opinion in still quite divided on the issue.

Opinion about marijuana legalization is very much a generational issue, and the older the American, the less likely the support for marijuana legalization. Pew Research Center reports that in its survey, support for marijuana legalization among the Silent Generation (those born 1928–1945) was only 29 percent, whereas support among millennials (those born 1981–1997) was 68 percent. Among baby boomers (those born 1946–1964), 50 percent support marijuana legalization, much like Generation Xers (those born 1965–1980), 52 percent of whom are supportive of legalizing the drug.

Opinion on the issue also varies according to demographics. Men favor legalization at a rate of 57 percent whereas only

49 percent of women favor it. Among white Americans, 55 percent favor marijuana legalization, compared with 58 percent of black Americans and 40 percent of Hispanic Americans. College actually makes people more likely to support marijuana legalization with 58 percent of those who have gone to college supporting legalization. Although, those with postgraduate education, favor marijuana legalization at a rate of 52 percent. Among those with only a high school education or less, only 47 percent are supportive and 51 percent think it should be illegal.

Pew also found that support for marijuana legalization differs according to political leanings. Whereas 59 percent of Democrats and 58 percent of Independents support marijuana legalization, Republicans polled the other way. Only 39 percent of Republicans want marijuana legal and 59 percent think it ought to be illegal.

There is at least one issue, however, where most Americans agree regardless of political affiliation. A full 59 percent of the population is opposed to the federal government enforcing federal laws against marijuana in states where the drug has been legalized for medical or recreational use. Opposition to federal involvement was highest among Independents at 64 percent, but federal involvement was also opposed at a high rate by both Republicans and Democrats, at 54 and 58 percent, respectively.

Pew reports that for those who do think marijuana should be legal, respondents differed in their main reason for support. The most common justification for supporting legalization was a belief in medicinal benefits (41 percent cited this as their main reason for support) followed by the belief that marijuana is not as dangerous as other drugs (36 percent cited this as their main reason). A little more than one-quarter, 27 percent, cited the benefits of regulation as their main reason for support, and 12 percent said they supported legalization because current enforcement is problematic.

Among the 44 percent who believe marijuana should be illegal, 43 percent said that they took this position based on the belief that marijuana hurts society or is bad for individuals. Almost one-third, 30 percent, cited a concern that marijuana was a dangerous, addictive drug. Others cited concerns about marijuana being a gateway drug and bad for young people.

Despite the majority support for legalizing marijuana, even the supporters do not favor the unbridled presence of marijuana, even if it were legal. Among those who favor marijuana legalization, 43 percent said that if marijuana were legal they would be bothered if people used marijuana in public. Supporters of legal marijuana were less worried about marijuana shops, with only 12 percent saying they would be bothered if a business selling marijuana opened in their neighborhood.

Opposing Viewpoints: The Legalization of Marijuana explores many controversial issues regarding legalizing the drug in chapters titled "Has the Prohibition Against Marijuana Been Successful?," "Is Marijuana Use Harmful?," "Should Use of Medical Marijuana Be Legal?," and "Should Recreational Use of Marijuana Be Legal?" The authors of the viewpoints within present different opinions on the issue of marijuana legalization, illustrating that although public opinion has moved in favor of legalization, the issue is far from settled.

OPPOSING
VIEWPOINTS®
SERIES

CHAPTER1

Has the Prohibition Against Marijuana Been Successful?

Chapter Preface

Prior to 1937, marijuana—specifically *Cannabis sativa*—was cultivated for use as an industrial fiber, medicine, and other uses with few federal restrictions in the United States. The Pure Food and Drug Act of 1906 required accurate labeling of marijuana sold as medicine but did not restrict its production, sale, or use. During the 1930s, however, public fear of marijuana increased; it was in 1936 that the film aggrandizing the harms of marijuana, *Reefer Madness*, was produced. The Marihuana Tax Act of 1937 placed a tax on the sale of marijuana, effectively restricting legal possession or transfer to authorized medical and industrial use. It criminalized possession of marijuana by individuals not authorized under the act. In the 1950s, stricter sentences for marijuana possession were enacted under the Boggs Act of 1951 and the Narcotics Control Act of 1956. These restrictions, however, did little to halt the growth in popularity of recreational marijuana use that became widespread in the 1960s.

The Controlled Substances Act (CSA) was passed as part of the Comprehensive Drug Abuse Prevention and Control Act of 1970. The CSA categorizes drugs by perceived risk of abuse and accepted medical uses, thereby making the manufacture, distribution, and possession of certain substances subject to federal regulation. Drugs such as heroin and marijuana are classified as having a high risk of abuse and no legitimate medical use. Such drugs are deemed Schedule I, and they are prohibited in all circumstances. Schedule II drugs, such as cocaine and certain prescription drugs, are considered as having a risk of abuse or dependence, but they also have medical uses and are available from a medical doctor. Schedule III, IV, and V drugs all must be dispensed by a medical practitioner and are determined to have less potential for abuse, with Schedule V drugs having the least potential for abuse.

A year after the CSA was passed, President Richard Nixon launched a new era of drug policy in the United States. In a White House speech he said, "America's public enemy number one in the United States is drug abuse. In order to fight and defeat this enemy, it is necessary to wage a new, all-out offensive." In 1973, the Drug Enforcement Administration (DEA) was created with an annual budget of less than $75 million. More than forty years later, that budget has increased to more than $2 billion.

Federal law regulates the criminal penalties that may be imposed for a conviction of a violation of marijuana prohibition. Penalties for marijuana trafficking across state lines, from outside the United States, or within the District of Columbia depend upon the quantity of marijuana and can be as stringent as life imprisonment. Penalties for simple marijuana possession at the federal level range from a fine to three years of imprisonment. In addition, there are mandatory minimum sentences for certain amounts and for repeat offenders. Criminal penalties for the manufacture, sale, and possession of marijuana at the state level vary widely, with each state having its own regulations.

As the authors of the viewpoints in the following chapter illustrate, there is wide disagreement about the wisdom and efficacy of marijuana prohibition as it has been implemented over the last several decades in the United States.

| *"Prohibition is an approach that needs to be replaced, not refined."*

Drug Prohibition Has Failed and Needs to End

Law Enforcement Against Prohibition

In the following viewpoint, Law Enforcement Against Prohibition (LEAP) argues that the current policy of prohibition of drugs engages law enforcement in policing activity that should not be criminal. LEAP contends that the prohibition of drugs itself is what creates many of the social problems surrounding illegal drug use. LEAP contends that regulation of marijuana and other drugs is the preferable policy. LEAP is a nonprofit organization made up of current and former members of law enforcement and criminal justice communities who are speaking out about the failures of existing drug policies.

As you read, consider the following questions:

1. According to LEAP, in what situation regarding drug use is the involvement of law enforcement justified?

2. Between 1993 and 2009, how many states legalized medical marijuana, according to the author?

Law Enforcement Against Prohibition, "After Prohibition," leap.cc, October 2013, pp. 3–4, 8–10, 13. Copyright © 2013 Law Enforcement Against Prohibition. All rights reserved. Reproduced with permission.

3. According to LEAP, how many Americans have used marijuana recreationally or medicinally at least once?

Law Enforcement Against Prohibition (LEAP) envisions a world in which drug policies work for the benefit of society and keep our communities safer. A system of legalization and regulation will decrease violence, better protect human rights, safeguard our children, reduce crime and disease, treat people suffering from drug abuse as patients rather than criminals, use tax dollars more efficiently, and restore the public's respect and trust in law enforcement.

Introduction

We are frontline warriors who have experienced, executed and examined the war on drugs. We started out as true believers and faithfully enforced drug laws until our consciences would no longer allow us to stay silent about the harms brought on by this war. We bear personal witness to the destructive futility of all drug prohibitions—from caffeine, tobacco and alcohol, to current bans on drugs that were once legal. Even if well intended, such prohibitions do not work and almost always harm the integrity of and respect for law enforcement.

America's increasing rejection of the corruption and violence that accompany prohibition is responsible for the game-changing response of the federal government to marijuana reform in Washington [State] and Colorado. But we appreciate the concern many feel about the accelerating pace of drug policy reform. What replaces prohibition? How will we protect our young?

Our report is aimed at those who are convinced of prohibition's terrible toll but who seek safe, workable alternatives. We know what happens when we arrest people for buying and using drugs. What happens when we don't?

This report contains:

1. A straightforward way to think about drugs that will allow us to move past a prohibition-only model;

2. Real-world examples of how moving away from prohibition reduces the rates of death, disease, crime and addiction; and

3. Specifics about what our drug policies and our communities might look like after prohibition.

Section 1: The State and Drug Use

Drugs are processed or unprocessed substances that may be used to heighten or suppress emotions. They provide a rapid shortcut to euphoria, pain relief or a temporary escape from the challenges and responsibilities of everyday life. They have been used in one form or another in virtually every known society. Some, such as heroin and nicotine, have a high potential for physical addiction. All can be seriously abused, whether legal or illegal.

Our position is that drugs themselves, regardless of their very real potential for abuse, are not moral agents—inherently good or evil—and that adults have an inalienable right to place what they choose in their bodies.

We do not take this position lightly, for many of us have witnessed the ravages of drug abuse on individuals and their families.

But we take seriously the inalienable right of the individual to use the mood-altering chemical of their choice when there are no deleterious effects, and in cases of abuse, we are joined by a growing number of community and medical leaders who consider drug abuse not a sign of criminal immorality, but a personal mental health issue to be confronted by religious leaders, addiction specialists, social workers, family and friends.

Law enforcement, the punitive arm of the state, is not an appropriate responder, whether the drug use is a personal choice or a personal problem.

Where abuse of others by an intoxicated person is involved, law enforcement is indeed called for, not because of the drug use, but because of the antisocial behavior. Drug use is neither an excuse for nor responsible for that behavior. If it is part of an offender's pattern of dysfunction, they may be directed to relevant services as part of their restitution and rehabilitation, but they must be held accountable for their actions, whether intoxicated or not.

Just as the drugs themselves are chemicals with no intrinsic moral qualities, no drug automatically yields antisocial behavior. There is considerable violence associated with the marijuana trade, virtually none with the cigarette trade. That violence has nothing to do with the intrinsic qualities of either drug. As with Al Capone's reign of street terror, it is not the drugs themselves that cause the violence, it is the policy of prohibition.

Our position does not require us to say a single good thing about drugs currently prohibited. When our grandparents and great-grandparents had the wisdom to end alcohol prohibition in 1933, they didn't think for a minute that the drug in question was safe for children, nontoxic, non-addicting or unassociated with self-destructive or antisocial behavior. Quite the contrary. But its prohibition caused the same unnecessary death, disease, crime and addiction as today's prohibition and was equally futile in preventing the prohibited behavior. It just made the drug in question more dangerous than it otherwise would be if legal and regulated rather than pushed underground.

Section 2: Local Efforts, Global Success

Prohibition is not just destructive and wasteful. As experienced law enforcement professionals, we know that it is temporary; a realization that is fast becoming commonsense wisdom. And so, despite ongoing American pressure, many countries have taken big, revealing steps away from criminalization. There are currently twenty-three countries with some form of drug decriminalization, and that number is sure to increase. Domestically, many states are also boldly shedding their prohibitionist laws.

What follows is a brief glimpse into the real-world good news that occurs every time we begin the move away from prohibitionist policies.

Portugal

In response to a dramatic rise in drug use and abuse in the 1990s, Portugal decided to treat drug abuse as a mental health problem instead of a criminal problem. Though selling remained illegal, possession of up to a 10-day supply of any drug, including heroin, is no longer a criminal offense for adults 18 and older. Dire predictions were made about the impact this would have on Portuguese youth.

Portugal provides a meaningful glimpse into a post-prohibition world in which heavy users are encouraged, but rarely forced, to seek treatment. Drug use doesn't magically disappear in this world any more than it ever has or ever will. But no worst fears were realized, and in fact there is much to celebrate and imitate. The bad stats declined. The good stats increased.

Drug use declined in every age category, but the younger ages showed the most reduction, and those are the ones we most need to affect if we are to stop feeding this monster of addiction. For children between the ages of 13 and 15, drug use declined by 25 percent and for young people between the ages of 16 and 18, it declined by 22 percent.

In 2000, 23 percent of first-time treatment clients were over 34 years old. In 2008, that number jumped to 46 percent.

Addiction specialists see this as evidence that fewer young people are becoming drug dependent, which is exactly the goal of good drug policy.

Disease and crime. The number of cases of HIV reported by intravenous drug users also decreased, by 71 percent; and the number of new AIDS cases dropped by 79 percent. This reflects the fact that harm reduction approaches such as needle exchange are most effective when there is an absence of police prosecution.

The proportion of offenses committed under the influence of drugs and/or to fund drug consumption dropped by half. Overall, there has been a clear reduction in the burden on the criminal justice and health care systems.

Treatment. The number of drug users in treatment jumped 62 percent between 1998 and 2008. Not because there were more drug users. There were not. This reflects the move from the criminal to the medical approach to drug addiction. When addicted people are no longer afraid of being arrested, if they seek help, many more will come forward and request that help. And when you are not spending tax money on arresting and imprisoning these people, you have money to spend on rehabilitative facilities. Portugal has increased its treatment programs by 300 percent, and it is weaning much of the addicted population off drugs.

Since decriminalizing all drugs for adults, Portugal has experienced a reduction in blood-borne diseases, "drug-related" crime, youthful drug use and youthful drug addiction. It also saw an increase in people getting treatment for their addiction—the foundation of a virtuous cycle in which lives are changed and saved.

Vancouver

In response to the increasing death, disease, crime and addiction caused by the unregulated abuse of opiates and other substances, Vancouver set up a supervised injection facility,

"Insite," where addicted people bring and use their own drugs under the supervision of medical personnel in a setting that encourages them to kick their addiction. This is one of a growing number of facilities (92 throughout the world), all of which have prevented countless overdose deaths and given hope to afflicted individuals, their families and communities. The following are the findings of Dr. Thomas Kerr, who performed an independent evaluation of this program. Not only were there universally positive outcomes from this medical approach to substance abuse, but there were no negative outcomes, despite dire predictions and initial opposition. Insite is now supported by the local police, the Canadian Medical Association and local merchants. It is proof positive that helping rather than hurting those suffering from chemical addiction is humane, cost effective, and possible.

Switzerland

In the late 1980s and early 1990s, Switzerland faced an intense problem of drug abuse, particularly of heroin, and growing numbers of HIV/AIDS cases from intravenous users sharing needles that elevated Switzerland to the highest rate of those terrible blood-borne diseases of any country in Europe. After careful study, the Federal Office of Public Health made an explicit decision in 1994 to address dependent drug use as a health problem rather than a crime problem. As part of this shift, they developed an experiment to treat heroin addicts with government-manufactured heroin. They also authorized methadone programs, safe injection rooms and needle exchange programs across the country, including in prisons. Each program was designed to allow for careful, evidence-based evaluation.

Dramatic decrease in death, disease, crime, and addiction. In more than twenty years, this program has not had one heroin overdose death. The program resulted in a 60 percent drop in felony crimes committed by patients, with an average 80 percent drop for those who have been in the program for at least one year. Rates of HIV and hepatitis among drug users have plummeted; now listing Switzerland as having the lowest rates of any country in Europe. Moreover, there was significant improvement in health outcomes for patients, including significantly reduced consumption of heroin and cocaine. Twenty percent of those in the Swiss program have quit using any illicit drug at all. The United States experiences far worse outcomes from our rehabilitative facilities, with only three to five percent of those folks quitting illicit drug use. And we only track our rehab graduates one year out, while the Swiss track their graduates five years out. The projects that treat heroin addiction by giving users government-issued heroin also realized a huge increase in patients who have returned to gainful employment.

The rate of new users of heroin decreased dramatically. Despite catastrophic warnings that helping addicts instead of prosecuting them "sends the wrong message," the Swiss programs led to a reduction in new heroin users. On June 2, 2006, the prestigious British medical journal, the *Lancet*, released a report on the Swiss project stating that over the past ten years Zurich has "seen an 82 per cent decline in new users of heroin." The reasons are complex, but many experts feel that two things are driving this decline in new users. The program makes heroin seem unattractive to young people because it is treating folks with a health problem, and there is less of a social opportunity to be introduced to heroin by the street dealers who have essentially been put out of business by this approach.

The pure, government-regulated heroin is provided to the patients on a sliding cost scale, so nearly everyone pays something for their drugs but if the patient has no money the heroin is free. That means heroin users no longer have to commit crimes to pay for their drugs. Also, because you can't beat "free," illicit heroin distributors are no longer in Swiss neighborhoods, rubbing shoulders with the young and enticing them into becoming the next statistic while trying to sell their illegal goods. Who would buy from illicit drug dealers selling unregulated drugs when they could be obtained from the government at little or no cost?

Governmental cost savings. This comprehensive public health approach has saved the country money in terms of court time, police time, reduced crime rates, smaller prison population, lowered demand for expensive health services, and a drop in the roles of those provided for by the state through welfare programs.

Widespread and growing support. In a 2008 referendum vote, the Swiss public affirmed this program by a large margin. Elements of the program have been emulated by seven countries: Germany, Denmark, Holland, Belgium, the United Kingdom, Spain and Canada.

The United States

An analysis of data from 1993 through 2009 by economists at three American universities found no evidence that legalized medical marijuana laws have contributed to more use of the drug by high school students.

During that time period, 13 states legalized medical marijuana. (Twenty-three states and the District of Columbia now have such a law, and legislation is pending in many others.)

Professor Benjamin Hansen of the University of Oregon, who studies risky behaviors, pointed out that "[i]n fact, the data often showed a negative relationship between legalization and marijuana use," meaning there was actually a decrease of use among teenagers when marijuana was legalized.

Researchers examined the relationship between legalization and various outcomes such as marijuana use at school, instances of drugs offered on school property, alcohol use and cocaine use. They found no evidence that legalization led to increases in marijuana use at school, the likelihood of being offered drugs on school property, or the use of other substances.

In addition to national Youth Risk Behavior Survey (YRBS) data, they drew on state YRBS data for 1993–2009 and data from the 1997 National Longitudinal Survey of Youth. They also examined the Treatment Episode Data Set, which contains information about whether patients at federally funded drug treatment facilities tested positive for marijuana upon admission. The results of this analysis suggested that the legalization of medical marijuana was unrelated to the likelihood that patients ages 15–20 tested positive for marijuana.

"We are confident that marijuana used by teenagers does not increase when a state legalizes medical marijuana," said Montana State's Professor D. Mark Anderson, an economics professor who studies health economics, risky behavior and crime.

Summary of Section 2

- Portugal's experience shows that people begin to move away from their addictions and unhealthy behaviors when the power of the state is not harnessed against them in a moralistic, harassing crusade.

- Vancouver and Switzerland show that the most effective way to deal with those addicted to hard drugs is not through punishment, but through a medical model of support in which physical addiction is isolated from the social problems thought to be caused by it, and non-judgmental help is provided.

- The American experience with medical marijuana suggests that people continue their own level of use; that no floodgates open when we allow people access to their previously forbidden medicines without the threat of arrest.

These reforms do not change the fact that under prohibition, cartels and street dealers still control the production, distribution and promotion of their products. Therefore, we can only get a glimpse of how much stronger and safer our nation could be once we abandon that approach. But as we move away from criminalization, good things happen—sometimes dramatically, sometimes incrementally.

Section 3: After Prohibition: Our Policies, Our Communities

Our policies. We know that reasonable people will disagree about regulation. Ongoing debates about the drinking age and allowable levels of cigarette promotion and taxation are examples of how the normal democratic process applies to drug policy. Once we remove the prohibition, that ongoing dialogue—local adjustments and preferences—can be applied to all drugs. We will then be positioned and empowered to meaningfully regulate and control them.

While this brief next section is not a rigid road map, it illustrates some directions policy might take. These are possible approaches to the regulation of drugs ranging from marijuana to heroin which permits flexibility and demands accountability.

For simplicity, we have divided our approach into two categories, one dealing with marijuana, and the other encompassing the full range of illegal drugs. Our fundamental point remains that prohibition should be repealed, not because of the relative safety of the drug in question, but because of the harms inherent in prohibitionist policies. Nonetheless, we make this division here because marijuana has achieved a separate status in drug policy discussions.

Marijuana. Despite decades of well-funded fearmongering and millions of arrests, marijuana is a plant that has been used recreationally or medicinally at least once by approximately 100,000,000 Americans. It seems reasonable and inevitable to treat marijuana as we do cigarettes or alcohol, though it will be easy to institute bans on overt marketing. It will be legal to grow, transport and sell the cannabis plant, subject to enforceable regulations, restrictions and taxation; just as we do with hops and barley or the tobacco plant. States currently providing the legwork on this transition can be used as models whose approaches will be accepted or modified as other states deem appropriate; just as we did when we ended alcohol prohibition.

Private production. Once the prohibition on growing marijuana is lifted, people will be allowed to cultivate this plant, just as people are allowed to brew their own beer, subject to local regulations. In some jurisdictions, the plants would have to be out of public view; in others, growers might have to register with the state; some would allow 3 plants, some would allow 14 plants, and so on.

Medical use. After prohibition, health providers will be free to set standards and restrictions that provide patients access to a plant that has been used medicinally for thousands of years and was part of the official medical pharmacopeia for most of our nation's history. It will be a subject of medical research on par with any other plant deemed by scientists to have medicinal potential.

General regulations. As with any drugs having consciousness-altering potential, there will be age limits and scientifically sound education about the potential downsides for young people. Impaired-driving laws will remain unchanged, but the mere presence of marijuana in hair samples, in the absence of other problematic behaviors, will not be grounds for arrest, on or off the road. Unlike alcohol, THC [tetrahydrocannabinol, the chief intoxicant in marijuana] remains in your system for weeks, and its presence is therefore not evidence of impairment. Environmental and labor regulations in effect for domestic and imported crops will now apply to the cannabis plant.

Heroin and other drugs. It is noteworthy that supervised injection sites were created in response to problems exasperated by addiction, not in the name of personal freedom, growth or exploration. Opiates and stimulants have a very high potential for damage and dependency and should, at a minimum, never be promoted for recreational use.

We share the concern about the widespread overuse of an array of stimulants and newly created synthetic drugs, regardless of their legal status. Yet we understand that there is nothing constructive in the prohibitionist approach to these drugs, and much that is destructive.

We know that homemade meth labs don't create demand for methamphetamine, but do cause horrific, unnecessary damage to producers and users alike. We know that crack cocaine functions like a poor person's Prohibition-era bathtub gin, magnifying the dangers inherent in the forbidden drug. We know that some truly dangerous synthetic drugs would have little reason to exist if their creators weren't in a perpetual cat-and-mouse game with law enforcement over the lag time of many months, if not years, between when those designer drugs are created and when they are officially made illegal. During that period, the new drugs can be sold without law enforcement interference. If all drugs were legal, no one would be creating additional designer drugs.

And, as with marijuana, there are viable alternatives. Successful cross-national experiences with the regulated distribution and consumption of the most dangerous drugs can be copied and modified when dealing with people whose lives are ruled, but not enhanced, by those drugs.

By bringing opiates and stimulants back into the legal system, we will ensure that the entire production and distribution chain, including doctor-supervised medicinal use, will include meaningful levels of governmental or clinical oversight. In order to partake of this tightly regulated market, for example, farmers from Afghanistan and other countries would have to be recognized as legitimate providers by their governments, thus reducing their vulnerability to terrorists who extort farmers by protecting them from prohibition-based government crackdowns. It will also allow law enforcement to get a meaningful handle on quantities and sources, both subjects vital to pursuing illegal diversion.

A very small percentage of the adult population will continue to want to try heroin or similar drugs at least once, and instead of finding street dealers, or friends who know street dealers, they will be able to go to highly regulated, specialized dispensaries and obtain limited amounts without sanction. Diversion to children will be treated with extreme severity and will be much easier to trace. Police who only have a finite amount of time will be much more capable of protecting our children from drug use once they are no longer charged with protecting every adult human being from themselves by decreeing what they can put in their own bodies.

In all such cases, the drugs would continue to be available. The addiction rate, virtually untouched by decades of intense prosecution, will remain roughly constant, likely dipping moderately.

But our approach to drugs and those who use them would change. And that, as we discuss next, will make all the difference.

"The likely cause of addiction has been discovered, and it is not what you think." Johann Hari makes that point in his new, groundbreaking book *Chasing the Scream: The First and Last Days of the Drug War.* For much of his life, Mr. Hari wrestled with the question, "What causes addiction?" Is it the "chemical hooks" in the drug itself that after say twenty days of steady use somehow latch onto your body and initiate a

craving that can't be overcome? Or is it a moral compass that is lacking in people who would use illicit drugs?

The idea that the drug's irresistible chemical properties cause the addiction found its supposed scientific basis in a study where rats were put in individual cages that contained two drinking bottles; one bottle held water, the other a solution of heroin or cocaine. In nearly every study, the rat would shun the water bottle and cleave to the bottle containing the drug, ingesting that substance until it died. This seemed proof of the claim that heroin and cocaine are addictive and will, in nearly every case, cause the user to experience death and destruction.

But in the 1970s Bruce Alexander, a professor of psychology in Vancouver, Canada, realized there was a problem with that study. The rat had been put in a cage alone, with nothing to do and no hope for any change. Professor Alexander began to wonder if it was the "addictive" drugs that made the animals ingest them until they died or whether it might be the environment the rat was assigned to that caused it to choose the drug solution over the water. To test his hypotheses, Professor Alexander created enclosures he called Rat Park. Rat Park contained everything a rat could possibly want: tunnels to run in, different kinds of foods to eat, toys to play with, other rats with which to socialize and have sex. And Rat Park had the requisite two bottles, one of water, the other with a solution of either heroin or cocaine. Mr. Hari reports that an interesting thing then happened.

"In Rat Park, all the rats obviously tried both water bottles, because they didn't know what was in them. But what happened next was startling.

"The rats with good lives didn't like the drugged water. They mostly shunned it, consuming less than a quarter of the drugs the isolated rats used. None of them died. While all the rats who were alone and unhappy became heavy users, none of the rats who had a happy environment did."

Wow. The experiment with Rat Park seemed to indicate that ending up with an addiction to a drug also requires an unhappy user. Now, Professor Alexander thought, if only we had some similar project that could be studied where human beings were captured in a caged environment and had a choice of ingesting water or a drug solution. Perhaps we could then solve the question of what causes addiction.

As it happened, we had exactly that situation occurring in Vietnam. "*Time* magazine," Mr. Hari points out, "reported using heroin was 'as common as chewing gum' among U.S. soldiers, and there is solid evidence to back this up: Some 20 percent of U.S. soldiers had become addicted to heroin there, according to a study published in the *Archives of General Psychiatry*. Many people were understandably terrified; they believed a huge number of addicts were about to head home when the war ended."

"But in fact," writes Mr. Hari, "some 95 percent of the addicted soldiers—according to the same study—simply stopped. Very few had rehab. They shifted from a terrifying cage back to a pleasant one, so didn't want the drug anymore."

The implications of this study are immense. For all these years we have been treating the effect and not the cause that makes people use drugs. If we can change their cages to something more palatable, we can cure this thing we call "drug addiction." We need to stop weaning folks off their drug of choice, then sending them back to exactly the same environment that caused them to want to use the drug in the first place.

The good news is that if we legalize and regulate these drugs we could, in the U.S. alone, save nearly 80 billion tax dollars that are spent every year on continuing the drug war. On top of that, according to Harvard economist Jeffrey Miron, we could raise an additional 44 billion dollars each year by taxing the sale of the newly legalized and regulated drugs.

© Copyright 2013 Adam Zyglis. All Rights Reserved.

If we spend that money on projects that give people hope for the future instead of spending it on removing any hope they may have through arrest and imprisonment, can you imagine how many fewer drug users we would have?

Our communities. Now that we have dismantled both the drug war and the drug cartels, and relieved many people of their need to use drugs, join us on a virtual "drive around" in our near-future patrol car to get a cop's sense of life on the streets . . . after prohibition.

We start out in our national parks and shake our heads when we think back on the gangs and cartels who had commandeered large swatches of land to grow marijuana when it was illegal. Incredible as it seems today, prohibition brought turf-protecting gang violence to our national parks. We also recall with some embarrassment the Keystone Cops videos of our comrades burning marijuana plants and looking as hapless as their predecessors who sternly smashed barrels of beer during the prohibition of alcohol. How our profession suffered under this policy!

We drive on, passing farmland revitalized by the legalized regulation of cannabis. Hemp has regained its colonial-days status as a patriotic American crop, requiring relatively little water, pesticide or fertilizer, providing environmentally safe paper, rope, clothing and more. The female plant that is associated with both recreational and medicinal use is being studied by virtually all medical centers, universities and drug companies. While common, cannabis farming is only moderately profitable, as it is easy to grow, and many small farmers supply [it for] themselves and their friends. We remember when it was obscenely profitable and a major source of untaxed funding for gangs and terrorists. Some of those gangs and terrorists remain, though profoundly weakened now that the vast majority of their income has disappeared. They have been hurt deeply by the fall of prohibition and many have been forced to seek legal employment, just as their bootlegging predecessors did after the prohibition of alcohol.

We drive on, into rural counties, where we pass a number of burnt-out houses and think sadly of the desperate people who lost everything from their amateur attempts to create the same methamphetamine safely manufactured by pharmaceutical companies. They, too, remind us of a dangerous past when people died making illegal alcohol when their homemade distilleries exploded. People are still using—and some abusing—that product, but of course without the punitive stigma of prohibition, it is easier and far more common for people to get help with their addiction.

We drive on, into the suburbs, where things seem remarkably unchanged. We pass the houses of successful people, some of whom are addicted to cocaine or heroin or alcohol. All have access to their drug of dependency, and when they use it they know what they are putting in their bodies and how much is too much. When it starts to affect their lives, they are able to find treatment.

We pass a school where some teens have decided that scraping bicycle tires and burning the rubber yields mood-altering smoke, and it has caught on among the bored and curious. As this fad passes through the nation, the media gamely labels it another "epidemic," but we know it will soon pass, though some kids will seriously, even fatally, damage their lungs. As we think back on the "Cinnamon Challenge" and other similar fads, we wish there was a way to legislate against impulsive stupidity. What we no longer see, though, is a large number of kids enlisted into the drug trade. Illegal activity is now less organized, more individual, smaller scale. It doesn't define or dominate the playground as it did during drug prohibition.

We pass by a hospital, and see women who successfully seek treatment for their addictions to painkillers or cocaine before becoming mothers. It is an affirming environment that encourages all women to avail themselves of prenatal care. This contrasts starkly with the previous generation, some of whom were forced to deliver in shackles (and often lost) their babies, not because they used child-endangering drugs such as cigarettes or alcohol, but because they used forbidden drugs. Illegal diversion still occurs, as happens now with oxycodone, but there is virtually no violence from prohibition-era turf battles over drug manufacture and sale; we law enforcers have reliable intelligence about the source and path of such drugs, unlike during the anarchy and chaos of prohibition. The addicted and their families and friends now have the resources to work together over time, a proven way to reduce addiction. Countless overdose deaths have been avoided because friends no longer fear calling 911 in the case of a bad drug reaction. Hospitals have slow days.

We drive on, into the inner city, where things are remarkably different. We immediately notice the increased number of men on the street, many having been released from prison as nonviolent drug "offenders" whose actions are no longer crimes and who were pardoned after review. As part of a restorative justice program, they receive remedial training to help them reintegrate into their shattered community. Their children walk with them, happy to have their fathers back. Nearly all of those among them who had been addicted to heroin are now drug free and gainfully employed because, years ago, we realized drugs do not cause addiction and their use is not a moral failing of the user; what addicts us is the cage. We have removed the cage.

Most notably, the statistics on gun and gang violence have dropped as dramatically as they did the year alcohol prohibition ended. Once they lost control of the illegal drug market, our modern gangs became shells of their former selves. Outlaws are no longer the role models they were during drug prohibition. While prostitution remains, pimps have lost their unique access to the drugs on which many of these women are dependent, and they have therefore lost much of their former absolute power.

Drug treatment clinics look the same as their inconspicuous European counterparts and they work just as effectively. Some former drug-runners work in those clinics or in regulated drug dispensaries, just as some former rum- and numbers-runners found legal employment in liquor stores or lottery outlets. They pay taxes, raise families, and vote. And life goes on.

We police are once again peace officers, our original name. We can pursue the rapists and child molesters who have been ignored because of monetary federal incentives to chase drug activities. As we drive down the street, kids look at us differently. Once we abandoned the stealth mode of undercover work required by an unenforceable prohibition, the community abandoned its "no-snitching" mentality. We are increasingly on the same team. It is, again, remarkably different.

We conclude our virtual drive at our multi-thousand-mile-long borders and shake our heads at the hundreds of thousands of deaths and the political instability that was caused by prohibition. We used to shrug when we heard drug warriors bragging about a five-ton bust, knowing that tens of tons of that same drug were simultaneously finding their way through the border. We are gratified that farmers are now allowed to grow crops, including poppies, as safely as they always grew other crops. And we are gratified that people, especially in the third world, have access to the pain relief that we take for granted but was formerly denied by drug prohibition. And, as with American street gangs, the cartels and terrorists who were empowered and armed by drug prohibition have at last suffered the deadly blow we tried to give them unsuccessfully for more than forty years.

Epilogue

Legalized regulation is not a panacea and will not end our very real drug problems. But it creates breathing room for personal redemption and community revitalization. It will cripple cartels and gangs, reduce street crime and deglamorize the outlaw drug dealer. And overall drug abuse will almost certainly decline as the afflicted are freed to pursue the long-term commitment required to defeat long-term addiction.

The message that legalized regulation sends is one of hope and support; one based on adult freedom and responsibility. We joined law enforcement to protect people from one another, not to monitor what they choose to ingest. If there is to be something called a "War on Drugs," it should be a war on drug abuse. And that war should only be fought as the successful war on tobacco addiction has been fought—with regulations such as education, targeted taxation, age restrictions, and limits on public usage, with clinics providing an array of help for the addicted.

Prohibition is an approach that needs to be replaced, not refined. And, as we have come to learn, that approach does not require a leap of faith.

Footnotes for this document can be found at http://bit.ly/1NY1bsd.

| "*Legalizing marijuana isn't going to fix national drug policy.*"

Marijuana Prohibition Policies Simply Need to Be Refined

Jamie Chandler and Skylar Young

In the following viewpoint, Jamie Chandler and Skylar Young argue that the problem with national drug policy is not the prohibition but the focus on demand-related policies. They argue that national marijuana policy ought to be shifted back toward supply-related prohibition, not toward legalization. Chandler is a political scientist at the Colin Powell School for Civic and Global Leadership at City College of New York and the Graduate School of Political Management at George Washington University. Young is a law student at the William S. Boyd School of Law at the University of Nevada, Las Vegas.

As you read, consider the following questions:

1. What is an example of a way in which marijuana proponents have used propaganda in promoting legalization, according to the authors?

2. Which US president shifted national drug policy from supply to demand, according to Chandler and Young?

Jamie Chandler and Skylar Young, "Legalizing Marijuana Won't End the War on Drugs," *U.S. News & World Report*, March 14, 2014. Copyright © 2014 U.S. News & World Report. All rights reserved. Reproduced with permission.

3. Which piece of legislation do the authors support in reforming US drug policy?

The success of any political movement depends on how well activists engineer consent. They must get a majority of the public to support their idea so that politicians jump on it and pass laws that make it a reality. Propaganda drives this process. It's the number one way to sway public opinion. People don't know much about politics, especially complex issues, so they tend to buy the hype.

Propaganda by Marijuana Proponents

We've got tons of recent examples of this. Birthers play on our tendency to believe conspiracy theories: As recently as 2010, 25 percent of the public doubted that President [Barack] Obama is a natural born citizen. Terms like "death panels" and "Obamacare" keep support for the [Patient Protection and] Affordable Care Act low: Nearly 54 percent oppose the law.

Propaganda isn't a bad thing. Edward Bernays, considered the father of public relations, said it's an essential part of a democratic society; but it does keep people from accurately perceiving issues.

Marijuana proponents are exceptional political marketers. Their Pot-aganda has convinced the public of the myths that marijuana hasn't killed anyone, isn't addictive and that medical marijuana is a wonder drug for treating epilepsy. They've also labeled opponents as morally judging pot smokers, which helps their message seem more credible.

Facts indicate otherwise. Marijuana is addictive; it's a gateway drug and marijuana-related fatal car accidents have tripled since 1999. Smokers inhale about 65 percent of pesticides found in marijuana buds and much of the evidence on medical marijuana and epilepsy is anecdotal.

The Harmful Effects of Marijuana

The immediate effects of taking marijuana include rapid heartbeat, disorientation, lack of physical coordination, often followed by depression or sleepiness. Some users suffer panic attacks or anxiety.

But the problem does not end there. According to scientific studies, the active ingredient in cannabis, THC [tetrahydrocannabinol], remains in the body for weeks or longer.

Marijuana smoke contains 50% to 70% more cancer-causing substances than tobacco smoke. One major research study reported that a single cannabis joint could cause as much damage to the lungs as up to five regular cigarettes smoked one after another. Longtime joint smokers often suffer from bronchitis, an inflammation of the respiratory tract.

Foundation for a Drug-Free World,
"The Truth About Marijuana," 2015.

Two Types of Prohibition

The biggest problem with pro-marijuana rhetoric is that its proponents seem to believe that legalization will end the war on drugs—naïve assertion that shows proponents fail to understand the complexities of why national drug [policy] isn't working.

President Richard Nixon declared a war on drugs in 1971, but his policy focused on supply. He targeted major drug cartels, and invested in drug treatment programs. President Ronald Reagan, on the other hand, shifted the policy to demand. His "get tough" and "zero tolerance policy" approaches locked up countless people for nonviolent drug offenses.

Reagan expanded funding for law enforcement, but cut it for drug treatment, prevention and education programs. Drug addicts became the enemy, and the 1980s crack epidemic made matters worse. "Zero tolerance" grew, and that was partly driven by implicit racism. The Anti-Drug Abuse Act of 1986 created mandatory sentencing standards that dramatically increased the African American prison population. Penalties for crack possession far exceeded those for cocaine. Politicians associated crack with low-income blacks and coke with middle-class whites.

Demand-side drug policy has remained the norm for the last 30 years and part of the reason is that it helps politicians reap electoral gains. Even today, President Barack Obama supports the drug war. Yes: he's made some pot-friendly remarks, but he likes the Edward Byrne [Memorial] Justice Assistance Grant Program. Although the [George W.] Bush administration practically defunded the program, Obama allocated $2 billion back to it with the American Recovery and Reinvestment Act of 2009. He wanted to convince the public that he was tough on crime. The program has a troubled history. It ties drug arrest statistics to funding: the more arrests, the more money. Most of the money goes to drug task forces that have a record of disproportionately arresting poor black men for possession.

The Need to Shift Policy

The first step to fix this problem is for Congress to pass S. 1410: Smarter Sentencing Act of 2014. The law would provide funding to reform sentencing rules, mitigate prison overcrowding and racial disparities and better identify dangerous drug offenders.

The bill has been stalled in committee for a year. And while it stands a decent chance of passing the Senate—some Republicans announced this week [in March 2014] that they're coming around to favoring it—it has zero chance of passing the GOP-controlled House. Republicans also like "tough on crime" policies.

Legalizing marijuana isn't going to fix national drug policy. Drug cartels will make money by shifting their focus to harder drugs or looking for new markets into which to smuggle pot. If we want to reform national drug policy, we're going to have to shift its focus back on supply, and push politicians to do a lot more than jump on the pro-pot bandwagon.

The most important thing is we need to get the marijuana legalization debate off spin and on substance. If we don't design drug policies around the lessons learned from the failure of the war on drugs, we're just going to get more shoddy policies that don't benefit the common good.

> "Whites and blacks use marijuana
> equally, but the police do not arrest
> them equally."

The Scandal of Racist Marijuana Arrests—and What to Do About It

Harry Levine

In the following viewpoint, Harry Levine argues that arrests for marijuana possession in the United States are skewed by race. Levine contends that studies show that young minorities are arrested at a much higher rate than young white people, even though rates of marijuana use are similar. He claims that only legalization, not merely decriminalization, will eliminate this particular effect of institutionalized racism. Levine is a professor of sociology at Queens College, City University of New York, and coauthor of Marijuana Arrest Crusade: Racial Bias and Police Policy in New York City, 1997–2007.

As you read, consider the following questions:

1. According to Levine, approximately how many arrests for marijuana possession have been made annually over the past fifteen years?

Harry Levine, "The Scandal of Racist Marijuana Arrests—and What to Do About It," *Nation*, November 18, 2013. Copyright © 2013 The Nation Company, LLC. All rights reserved. Used by permission and protected by the Copyright Laws of the United States. The printing, copying, redistribution, or retransmission of this Content without express written permission is prohibited.

2. The war on drugs shifted its focus from cocaine to marijuana in what decade and under what US president, according to the author?

3. Levine contends that what two states have made the right move in legalizing marijuana?

"Whites Smoke Pot, but Blacks Are Arrested." That was the headline of a column by Jim Dwyer, the great Metro desk reporter for the *New York Times*, in December 2009. Although Dwyer was writing about New York City, he summed up perfectly two central and enduring facts about marijuana use and arrests across the country: Whites and blacks use marijuana equally, but the police do not arrest them equally. A third important fact: The vast majority (76 percent) of those arrested and charged with the crime of marijuana possession are young people in their teens and 20s.

Over the last fifteen years, police departments in the United States made 10 million arrests for marijuana possession—an average of almost 700,000 arrests a year. Police arrest blacks for marijuana possession at higher rates than whites in every state and nearly every city and county—as FBI [Federal Bureau of Investigation] Uniform Crime Reporting and state databases indisputably show. States with the largest racial disparities arrest blacks at six times the rate of whites. This list includes Alabama, Illinois, Iowa, Kansas, Kentucky, Minnesota, Pennsylvania, Nebraska, Nevada, New York and Wisconsin.

Big city police departments are among the worst offenders. Police in Los Angeles, Chicago and New York have arrested blacks for marijuana possession at more than seven times the rate of whites. Since 1997, New York City alone has arrested and jailed more than 600,000 people for possessing marijuana; about 87 percent of the arrests are of blacks and Latinos. For years, police in New York and Chicago have arrested more young blacks and Latinos for simple marijuana possession than for any other criminal offense whatsoever.

Other large urban areas that make huge numbers of racially biased arrests include Atlanta, Baltimore, Buffalo, Cleveland, Dallas-Fort Worth, Detroit, Fort Lauderdale, Houston, Las Vegas, Memphis, Miami, Nashville, Philadelphia, St. Louis, Tampa and Washington, DC. And across the United States, one-third of marijuana arrestees are teenagers; 62 percent are age 24 or younger; and most of them are ordinary high school or college students and young workers.

The essential study of these possession arrests and their pervasive racial bias is "The War on Marijuana in Black and White," an extraordinary book-length report released by the ACLU [American Civil Liberties Union] earlier this year [2013]. It found that police arrest blacks for marijuana possession at higher rates than whites in poor, middle-class and wealthy communities (with richer counties showing the greatest bias). The glaring racial disparities in marijuana arrests are "as staggering in the Midwest as in the Northeast, in large counties as in small, on city streets as on country roads. . . . They exist regardless of whether blacks make up 50% or 5% of a county's overall population."

Young whites (age 18 to 25), however, use marijuana more than young blacks, and government studies comparing marijuana use among whites and blacks of all ages have found that both groups use it at a similar rate.

Why are marijuana arrests so racially skewed? Such dramatic and widespread racial disparities are clearly not the product of personal prejudice or racism on the part of individual police officers. This is not a problem of training or supervision or rogue squads or bad apples. It's a systemic problem, a form of institutional racism created and administered by people at the highest levels of law enforcement and government.

Most people arrested for marijuana possession were *not* smoking it: They typically had a small amount hidden in their clothing, vehicle or personal effects. The police found the marijuana by stopping and searching them (often illegally), or by tricking them into revealing it.

Police departments concentrate their patrols only in certain neighborhoods, usually ones designated as "high crime." These are mainly places where low-income whites and people of color live. In these neighborhoods, police stop and search the most vehicles and individuals while looking for "contraband" of any type to make an arrest. The most common item that people in any neighborhood possess that will get them arrested—and the most common item that police find—is a small amount of marijuana.

Police officers patrolling in middle- and upper-middle-class neighborhoods typically do not search the vehicles and pockets of white people, so most well-off whites enjoy a de facto legalization of marijuana possession. Free from the intense surveillance and frequent searches that occur in other neighborhoods, they have little reason to fear a humiliating arrest and incarceration. This produces patterns, as in Chicago, where whites constitute 45 percent of the population but only 5 percent of those arrested for possession.

The result has been called "racism without racists." No individual officers need harbor racial animosity for the criminal justice system to produce jails and courts filled with black and brown faces. But the absence of hostile intent does not absolve policy makers and law enforcement officials from responsibility or blame. As federal judge Shira Scheindlin recently determined in two prominent stop-and-frisk cases, New York City's top officials "adopted an attitude of willful blindness toward statistical evidence of racial disparities in stops and stop outcomes." She cited the legal doctrine of "deliberate indifference" to describe police and city officials who "willfully ignored overwhelming proof that the policy . . . is racially discriminatory and therefore violates the United States Constitution."

Racially biased marijuana enforcement stretches far beyond New York City—and its pernicious effects extend far beyond the degrading experience of being arrested and jailed. Most serious are the lifelong criminal records produced by a single arrest. Twenty years ago, misdemeanor arrest records were papers stored in dusty file cabinets. Now they are computerized and instantly available for $20 or less from commercial database firms—and easily found by a Google search for the phrase "criminal records." (Try it yourself.) Employers, landlords, schools, banks and credit card companies rule out applicants on the basis of these now universally available records, which have been aptly described as a "scarlet letter" and a "new Jim Crow." The substantial damage caused by criminal records from the millions of marijuana arrests has also been willfully disregarded by top officials almost everywhere, including in Congress and the White House.

Perhaps surprisingly, police departments, prosecutors and elected officials rarely discuss their marijuana arrests. They don't take credit for—or try to justify—arresting and jailing people in record-breaking numbers for possession. In fact, they usually seek to keep marijuana arrests out of the public eye.

This makes it difficult for many white Americans to believe that so many people are being arrested for possessing small amounts of marijuana. The news media don't report on these cases; nor are white Americans likely to personally know anyone who has been arrested (or whose children have been arrested) for marijuana possession. To an extraordinary extent, middle-class and especially upper-middle-class and wealthy white Americans have been shielded from information about—and remain unaffected by—the policing of marijuana possession. The near invisibility of these arrests has also hidden the strong support for them by police departments and prosecutors.

The national crusade against marijuana can be traced to the early 1990s, as the "war on drugs" shifted its focus from crack cocaine to marijuana under Bill Clinton. Since then, Congress has regularly allocated billions in federal funding to local police and prosecutors under the Justice Department's antidrug and police programs. Grantees often report their drug possession arrests as evidence of their accomplishments using these funds—and as proof that they should receive more. Federal money has thus subsidized the arrests of millions of young people for possessing marijuana, disproportionately young people of color. Prominent blue-state Democrats like Joe Biden, Dianne Feinstein, Charles Schumer, Hillary Clinton and Barack Obama have strongly supported these grants over the years; in 2009, the fiscal stimulus actually doubled the antidrug funding for local law enforcement agencies.

More than many people realize, prominent liberals have long been among law enforcement's most important political allies. A substantial power bloc of "drug war liberals"—or what might more broadly be termed "law-and-order liberals"—has played a major role in sustaining this drug war policing. Police departments depend on liberal Democrats to defend their funding and policy needs. Liberals in Congress and the White House, in turn, depend on police lobbying groups to support important legislation, such as their endorsement of immigration and gun reforms. And politicians at all levels of government gain credibility with many voters by having top police officials vouch for their steadfastness in "fighting crime."

With this federal support and encouragement, arrests for marijuana possession climbed from a crack-era low of 260,000 in 1990, to 500,000 in 1995, to 640,000 in 2000, to 690,000 in 2005, to 750,000 in 2010. The ACLU calculates that these arrests have cost taxpayers at least $3.6 billion a year. And there is absolutely no evidence that they reduce serious or violent crime—or even drug use.

So the question again becomes: Why? Why have these millions of arrests happened? Why is it so hard to stop them? While federal funding and drug war propaganda have helped drive marijuana arrests, police and sheriffs' departments have had their own reasons to embrace and fiercely defend the practice. Central to understanding the national marijuana arrest crusade is the fact that significant constituencies within police departments benefit from marijuana arrests, find them useful for internal departmental purposes, and want them to continue.

For ordinary patrol officers, marijuana arrests are relatively safe and easy work. Policing can be dangerous, but officers are unlikely to get shot or stabbed while searching and arresting teenagers for marijuana possession. All police departments have formal and informal activity quotas; in many departments, officers can show productivity and earn overtime pay by stopping and searching ten or so young people near the end of a shift and making a marijuana arrest. Police officers in New York have long used the term "collars for dollars" to refer to the practice of making misdemeanor arrests to earn overtime pay. Also, from the officers' point of view, people possessing marijuana are highly desirable arrestees. As one veteran lieutenant put it, they are "clean"; unlike drunks and heroin addicts, young marijuana users rarely have HIV, hepatitis, tuberculosis or even body lice. They are unlikely to throw up on the officer, in the patrol car or at the station. Marijuana arrests are indeed a quality-of-life issue—for the police.

Most important, police department supervisors at all levels find that marijuana possession arrests are very useful. They are proof of productivity to their superiors; some supervisors also receive overtime pay for the extra work by officers under their command. Making many searches and arrests for minor offenses is also excellent training for rookie police. If a new officer screws up the paperwork, it doesn't matter because, as one sergeant explained, "it's just a pot arrest." And if a crisis or emergency comes up, police commanders can temporarily

The War on Marijuana

The war on marijuana has largely been a war on people of color. Despite the fact that marijuana is used at comparable rates by whites and blacks, state and local governments have aggressively enforced marijuana laws selectively against black people and communities. In 2010, the black arrest rate for marijuana possession was 716 per 100,000, while the white arrest rate was 192 per 100,000. Stated another way, a black person was 3.73 times more likely to be arrested for marijuana possession than a white person—a disparity that increased 32.7% between 2001 and 2010. It is not surprising that the war on marijuana, waged with far less fanfare than the earlier phases of the drug war, has gone largely, if not entirely, unnoticed by middle- and upper-class white communities.

In the states with the worst disparities, blacks were on average over six times more likely to be arrested for marijuana possession than whites. In the worst offending counties across the country, blacks were over 10, 15, even 30 times more likely to be arrested than white residents in the same county. These glaring racial disparities in marijuana arrests are not a northern or southern phenomenon, nor a rural or urban phenomenon, but rather a national one.

American Civil Liberties Union (ACLU),
"The War on Marijuana in Black and White," June 2013.

reassign officers making arrests for marijuana without hindering an ongoing investigation. This "reserve army" of police focusing on petty offenses keeps officers busy, provides records of their whereabouts and productivity, and gives commanders staffing flexibility.

Marijuana arrests also enable police department managers to obtain fingerprints, photographs and other data on young people who would not otherwise end up in their databases. There is nothing else the police can do that gets so many new people into their system as the broad net of marijuana possession arrests.

Police officials and managers have become so dependent on marijuana arrests that one could reasonably conclude that their departments are addicted to them. And they don't want to give up their habit. In recent years, police agencies, prosecutors' offices, and their influential network of political and lobbying organizations have emerged as the chief opponents of drug law reform. It is not the religious right, or antidrug groups, or even the drug treatment industry that lobbies and campaigns against marijuana ballot initiatives and legislative drug law reforms. Rather, law enforcement organizations are leading the charge as well as providing the troops to defend the drug war.

The ACLU's report emphatically calls for an end to marijuana possession arrests, noting that the only way to accomplish this is by legalizing the possession and use of marijuana, and ultimately by regulating its production and sale.

Although the decriminalization of marijuana possession has been implemented in countries with a national police system, in the United States this has turned out to be a false solution. When possession becomes a "noncriminal" offense but still an illegal one, local law enforcement agencies often continue many of the same practices as before—but now without public defenders to represent the young people charged with a "drug offense," and without public data to document what police, prosecutors and courts are doing. Some police departments simply ignore the decriminalization laws, as the NYPD [New York City Police Department] has done for over fifteen years.

However, as Colorado and Washington [State] have proved in just the last year, there is a very good alternative: Even without instituting commercial sale, the legalization of marijuana can stop most of these possession arrests.

The larger goal of ending punitive and biased drug arrests requires seismic changes in law enforcement: It will mean creating policing for a post–drug war America. One reform that makes others possible is guaranteeing public access to much more aggregate criminal justice data, both historical and current. With it, researchers and journalists can reveal routine police, prosecutor and court practices, as some of us have been doing for marijuana arrests and stop-and-frisks.

One way of conceptualizing these changes is to view them as bringing the civil rights movement to policing policies. In the last two decades, police department staffs have become increasingly racially integrated. But in many cities and counties, the day-to-day practices of police and sheriffs' departments are still determined by the race, class and ethnicity of a neighborhood's residents. Despite the many successes of the civil rights movement, we continue to live within two worlds of policing, separate and unequal: one for middle-class and wealthier people, the other for poorer Americans and, especially, people of color.

It is time for America to fully embrace equal policing for all. Unfortunately, like all humane, just and progressive change, this will not be granted. It must be won.

"Police enforce low-level drug offenses in high-crime areas because they are try-ing to establish norms of lawful con-duct."

Pot Possession and the Police

Heather Mac Donald

In the following viewpoint, Heather Mac Donald argues that marijuana arrests are higher in high-crime neighborhoods be-cause there is a greater police presence there to help fight crime. She claims that the fact that these neighborhoods are often largely minority neighborhoods, not racism, explains why marijuana ar-rests are higher for black and Hispanic young people. Mac Don-ald contends that any decriminalization of private marijuana use should not interfere with proactive policing. Mac Donald is the Thomas W. Smith Fellow at the Manhattan Institute for Policy Research and a contributing editor of City Journal.

As you read, consider the following questions:

1. According to the author, what laws governed marijuana possession in New York City up until Andrew Cuomo's proposed bill?

Heather Mac Donald, "Pot Possession and the Police," City-journal.org, June 7, 2012. Copyright © 2012 Manhattan Institute for Policy Research. All rights reserved. Repro-duced with permission.

2. According to Mac Donald, what percentage of shootings and violent crimes in New York are committed by black and Latino individuals?

3. How many minority lives have been saved since New York started its proactive policing revolution, according to the author?

New York governor Andrew Cuomo has introduced a bill into the state legislature that drastically reduces the penalty for the public possession of small amounts of marijuana. The law represents Cuomo's entry into an escalating controversy over the New York City Police Department's stop-and-frisk practices: Anti-cop advocates charge that racially biased stop-and-frisks are producing racially biased marijuana arrests. Neither charge is true, and Cuomo's failure to say so has done the city a disservice. Nevertheless, Cuomo's bill is a change the city can live with, one that may even produce public safety benefits. Predictably, however, the NYPD's opponents have already made clear that the proposed marijuana law will have no effect on their crusade to decimate proactive policing once and for all.

Until now, New York's marijuana laws have made the following distinctions: Possession of less than 26 grams of marijuana (7/8th of an ounce) was a violation, subject only to a summons and fine—so long as the marijuana was out of public sight. ("Violations" are not "crimes" under the state penal code, though they are still illegal.) Smoking marijuana in public, however, or possessing a small amount in public view was a misdemeanor crime for which the offender could be arrested. This distinction was a reasonable accommodation with the pro-legalization movement. It recognized that the public consumption or purchase of illegal drugs should be punished more heavily than private consumption, since the public flouting of the law is a greater threat to neighborhood order than private disobedience.

A sociologist at Queens College, though, has been promoting the idea that New York police officers deliberately use two illegitimate measures to jack up their arrests of young black and Hispanic males for public marijuana possession. In the first method, according to Professor Harry Levine, an officer somehow persuades young black and Hispanic males to take their concealed marijuana out of their pockets and display it in public in order to arrest them for public possession. In the second, an officer uncovers marijuana on a minority male in the course of a stop-and-frisk search and then makes a public-possession arrest. Such an arrest would not be legitimate: Possession of less than 26 grams of marijuana, discovered during a search, is a violation punishable by a $100 fine. It is not a misdemeanor.

Levine and his fans at the New York Civil Liberties Union and the *New York Times* have little data to support their allegation that officers have been engaging in the wholesale, unlawful arrest of blacks and Hispanics for small amounts of marijuana that only became public because of a search. The only statistic they can point to is the rise in marijuana possession arrests over the last 15 years. But the data do not even show that most of those possession arrests were for small amounts of marijuana, much less that the arrests were made because the police, in Levine's words, "intimidated or tricked" minority youth. Most of the 300,000 or so arrests for marijuana possession from 1997 to 2006 that Levine criticizes were for smoking in public or for possessing amounts ranging from 25 grams to 8 ounces. Only about 500 to 1,000 people were arrested annually over that period for public possession of under 26 grams.

Levine's charge that the police have been arresting young minorities in large numbers for public possession of marijuana revealed through a search rests ultimately only on the uncorroborated claims of Legal Aid Society attorneys and public defenders. The allegation has nevertheless become gospel truth in anti-cop circles. In response to the activists' pressure, Police Commissioner Ray Kelly circulated a departmental memo in September 2011 reaffirming the existing law: that less than 26 grams of marijuana discovered during a search did not constitute an arrestable crime. Legal Aid's Steve Banks and drug-legalization advocate Ethan Nadelmann hailed Kelly's memo as a major change of departmental rules, though it only restated long-standing policy.

Marijuana possession arrests dropped by nearly a quarter after Kelly's memo, according to the *Times*; how much of that drop occurred because some officers had in fact been making public-possession arrests after a search and now were no longer doing so, and how much was because the controversy regarding the issue had simply inhibited drug enforcement, is impossible to say. But any possession arrests that had been mistakenly made as a result of a search would never have been prosecuted, *pace* the advocates, nor would the arrest appear on someone's record. And the idea that the NYPD had a de facto policy of illegal arrests, or that officers set out to ruin minority lives, as City Council grandstanders have charged, is of course preposterous.

Cuomo's proposed law makes the public possession of less than 26 grams of marijuana a violation subject only to fine, not arrest—in effect, decriminalizing it. It would continue to allow the misdemeanor arrest of people smoking marijuana in public, which is why Commissioner Kelly and New York City mayor Mike Bloomberg support it. (By contrast, a bill proposed by Brooklyn assemblyman Hakeem Jeffries and Buffalo state senator Mark Grisanti would demote public smoking to violation status as well.) As a backstop to the existing law regarding marijuana discovered during a search, Cuomo's bill is clearly unobjectionable. The judgment is only slightly more difficult regarding marijuana observed on the street. Under Cuomo's revision, if someone is holding a joint weighing under 26 grams, but not smoking it, or even if he has just purchased that joint from a dealer, he can henceforth only be issued a summons, and cannot be arrested. (The person selling to him, however, can be arrested. In practice, drug enforcement rarely targets such small hand-to-hand transactions, to the extent that they happen at all. Dealers usually sell baggies containing amounts larger than 25 grams.)

Losing the opportunity to make arrests for public possession of small amounts of marijuana is worth the demolition of one of the more ubiquitous canards against the stop-and-frisk program—that it is being deliberately abused to arrest minorities. And the decriminalization law may even improve the NYPD's ability to police high-crime areas. It continues to allow the police to intervene in illegal behavior and to send the message to youth violating the law that the police are watching. Writing a summons is far less time-consuming than processing an arrest. The time officers save by not having to go to court for an arrest could increase patrol presence on the street and free them up for additional enforcement activity. Indeed, Harry Levine is already grousing that the 50,000 arrests could turn into 100,000 summonses.

The caveat, however, is that the justice system must follow through and make sure that offenders who have been summonsed are held accountable by paying their fines or doing their community service. If the courts don't take summons enforcement seriously, then the program could degenerate into a meaningless charade, with individuals giving fake identities and disappearing from view. Such was the fate of a reform in the 1970s and 1980s to expedite the processing of misdemeanor arrests through the issuance of "desk-appearance tickets." The city's district attorneys must ensure that the new marijuana violations are rigorously enforced, or Cuomo's bill could become the first step back to the chaos of earlier years.

Now that the police commissioner and mayor have acceded to Cuomo's desire to portray himself as a champion of "fairness," as he put it in a press conference, perhaps the governor could return the favor by rebutting the lies around crime and policing in the city. Here are a few places he could start:

Hot-spot policing, which includes stop-and-frisks, is not racist. The same day that the *Times* reported on Cuomo's proposed marijuana change, it ran an article about a fatal shooting on a Harlem basketball court; in fact, the two articles appeared side by side. Four young males (black, of course, though that detail was not disclosed) were shot while playing basketball at 4:50 p.m. Sunday; one of them, who had been shot in the back, was dead on arrival at the hospital. The *Times* and every professional cop critic in the city seem incapable of making the connection between such mindless violence and the fact that the NYPD concentrates its police resources in high-crime minority neighborhoods. It's highly improbable that anyone playing basketball on a Sunday afternoon in Battery Park City, say, would be shot to death. If such shootings *were* common, the police would flood that neighborhood with cops looking for suspicious behavior just as they do in Harlem and other high-crime areas. Race has nothing to do with the NYPD's tactics; the only determinant is crime.

Far from understanding this elemental truth about policing—one that its own coverage sometimes makes crystal clear, however inadvertently—the *Times* remains resolutely committed to the blatant untruth that the NYPD is engaged in biased policing. The day after the basketball-killing story, and next to its follow-up story on the Cuomo marijuana proposal, the *Times* announced that national gay groups would be calling on Mayor Bloomberg to end stop-and-frisks. "'We are all standing together against police harassment on the basis of a person's identity,'" Rea Carey, executive director of the National Gay and Lesbian Task Force, told the *Times* in an interview. To buttress Carey's claim that the police were "harassing" people based on racial "identity," the *Times* trotted out its favorite statistic: In 2011, "87 percent of those stopped were black or Latino." Its next sentence in the print edition was a classic: "The Police Department, its commissioner, Raymond W. Kelly, and the Bloomberg administration have repeatedly argued that the practice has been effective at preventing crime and saving lives." (The web edition added a clause about minorities being the majority of homicide and shooting victims.) Implication: Yes, we are targeting stops based on a "person's identity," but "the practice" is "effective." The sentence that logically *should* have followed the racial-stop statistic was: 98 percent of all shootings and 92 percent of all violent crimes are committed by blacks and Latinos, usually in minority neighborhoods. But you will never see those numbers in the *Times.*

Even more outrageously, the *Times* called last month for the Department of Justice to investigate the NYPD for its treatment of minorities. Never mind that there is not a more restrained and tightly managed department in the country. New York officers shot and killed 8 people in 2010—fewer than at any time since the department began collecting data in 1971 and down 33 percent from 2009. The number of times officers discharge their weapons was also at a new low. Attorney General Eric Holder and Department of Justice career attorneys have nothing to offer the NYPD when it comes to effective and fair policing.

Marijuana arrests are not racist. Harry Levine, the *Times,* and the New York Civil Liberties Union trumpet the fact that most arrestees for low-level marijuana crimes in New York City are black and Hispanic, even though national polls allegedly show that young whites use marijuana at higher rates than young minorities. Those national polls are based on self-reporting; they don't measure frequency of consumption or whether that consumption occurs in public or private. Let us assume for the moment that New York City displays the same patterns of marijuana use as nationally. Let us even assume that white teens walk down the street smoking joints at the same rate as black teens (something that does not conform to my informal observations, though the recent arrival in New York of the loathsome white gutter punks who have colonized sidewalks on the West Coast may change that).

The reason that marijuana arrests are higher in high-crime neighborhoods is that their law-abiding residents ask for heavier police presence and for enforcement of all the laws—including drug laws. The anti-cop advocates love to point out that the 50,000 marijuana-possession arrests in 2011 were more than all such arrests in the 19 years leading up to 1996, when marijuana arrests began rising under the mayoral administration of Rudolph Giuliani. Recall what those 19 years were like: "Twenty years ago you couldn't walk through here," a 58-year-old former junkie told me at an East Harlem anti-stop rally several weeks ago. "There's no crime here anymore." From 1977 to 1996, those allegedly halcyon days without marijuana enforcement, 12.4 million felonies were committed in the city; from 1997 to 2006, there were only 2.6 million. And it was minority neighborhoods in those pre-Giuliani decades that were most lethally overrun by both crime and the drug trade. Police enforce low-level drug offenses in high-crime areas because they are trying to establish norms of lawful conduct. Ideally, parents would be the ones enforcing those norms, but when they fail to, as the predation in minority neighborhoods shows has happened, the police will step in in their stead.

New York is the safest big city in the country thanks to proactive policing. New Yorkers are oblivious to the gulf that separates the city's crime portrait from that of every other metropolis with a large minority population. Gotham's crime drop has been twice as deep and has lasted twice as long as the national crime drop that began in the mid-1990s. No other urban area comes close. The cause of that crime drop was the policing revolution that began in 1994 under Mayor

Rudolph Giuliani and Police Commissioner William Bratton, as the University of California's Franklin Zimring argues in his recent book, *The City That Became Safe*. The NYPD's critics are forever trying to put forth alternative models of policing that the NYPD should emulate. These comparisons are, frankly, a joke. Chicago, which has traditionally shunned proactive stop-and-frisks, is a favorite of Columbia University's Jeff Fagan and Yale's Tracey Meares, both regular sources for the *New York Times*. In 2010, Chicago's murder rate was more than double that of New York; juveniles under the age of 17 are killed in the Windy City at four times the rate of those in New York. A recent *Times* op-ed proposed the policing strategies of Boston and High Point, North Carolina, as replacements for the NYPD's hot-spot policing. Boston's crime rate is 4,107 crimes per 100,000 residents; High Point's is 5,212 crimes per 100,000 residents; New York's is 2,257 crimes per 100,000 residents. Thank you, but I'll stick with the NYPD.

After demonstrating in *The City That Became Safe* that nothing else besides assertive policing explains why the NYPD's crime accomplishments trounce every other department, Zimring concludes, with obvious reluctance, that the large drop in violent death and imprisonment among minority males in New York City is "probably" more important than the high rate of stops and misdemeanor arrests, including for marijuana offenses, among minority youth. Let those of us unencumbered by academic inhibitions be clearer: The over 10,000 minority lives that have been saved since the onset of New York's policing revolution are unequivocally more important than an elevated risk of getting stopped, including for marijuana violations, in a high-crime neighborhood.

Governor Cuomo has grabbed national headlines for his marijuana proposal. Good for him. If he really wanted to show leadership, however, he should also state the obvious: that the NYPD is the best government program yet devised for bringing to the city's poor the right to life and freedom from fear. These are, after all, the most fundamental human rights of all.

"The arbitrary criminalization of tens of millions of Americans who consume marijuana results in a large-scale lack of respect for the law and the entire criminal justice system."

Marijuana Prohibition Is Ineffective and Unpopular

Marijuana Policy Project

In the following viewpoint, the Marijuana Policy Project (MPP) argues that the prohibition of marijuana has not been successful in keeping marijuana out of the hands of Americans and has resulted in hundreds of thousands of needless arrests. MPP claims that patients and doctors support the legalization of medical marijuana and the majority of Americans support the legalization of recreational marijuana. By legalizing marijuana, MPP contends that the negative effects of prohibition will be avoided. MPP is an organization that aims to change laws to eliminate prohibition of the medical and nonmedical use of marijuana.

As you read, consider the following questions:

1. How many marijuana arrests have there been in the United States since 1995, according to the author?

Marijuana Policy Project, "Marijuana Prohibition Facts," Mpp.org. Copyright © Marijuana Policy Project. All rights reserved. Reproduced with permission.

2. Which four states have enacted measures making marijuana legal for adults aged twenty-one and over, according to the Marijuana Policy Project?

3. According to the author, how many people have been killed since 2006 in Mexican drug cartel–related violence?

Relatively few Americans had even heard about marijuana when it was first federally prohibited in 1937. Today, over 106 million Americans admit to having tried it, and over 17.4 million say they have used it in the past month.

According to government-funded researchers, high school seniors consistently report that marijuana is easily available, despite decades of a nationwide drug war. With little variation, every year over 80% consider marijuana "fairly easy" or "very easy" to obtain.

The Criminal Sanctions

There have been more than 12 million marijuana arrests in the United States since 1995, including more than 693,000 in 2013, significantly more than for all violent crimes combined. One person is arrested for marijuana every 51 seconds. More than 87% of all marijuana arrests are for possession—not manufacture or distribution.

Every comprehensive, objective government commission that has examined marijuana use and its prohibition throughout the past 100 years has recommended that adults should not be criminalized for using marijuana.

Cultivation of even one marijuana plant is a federal felony.

Lengthy mandatory minimum sentences apply to myriad offenses. For example, a person must serve a five-year mandatory minimum sentence if federally convicted of cultivating 100 marijuana plants—including seedlings or bug-infested, sickly plants. This is longer than the average sentences for auto theft and manslaughter!

A one-year minimum prison sentence is mandated for "distributing" or "manufacturing" controlled substances within 1,000 feet of any school, university, or playground. Most areas in a city fall within these "drug-free zones." An adult who lives three blocks from a university is subject to a one-year mandatory minimum sentence for selling an ounce of marijuana to another adult—or even growing one marijuana plant in his or her basement.

In 2006, the last year for which data is available, federal government figures indicated there were more than 41,000 Americans in state or federal prison on marijuana charges, not including those in county jails. That's more than the number imprisoned on all charges combined in eight individual European Union countries.

A federal survey found that nearly 10% of former state prison inmates had been sexually victimized the last time they were incarcerated. Females were three times more likely to be victimized by other inmates than males, and 39% of gay male inmates were victimized by other inmates.

Civil forfeiture laws allow police to seize the money and property of suspected marijuana offenders—charges need not even be filed. The claim is against the property, not the defendant. The owner must then prove that the property is "innocent." Enforcement abuses stemming from forfeiture laws abound.

According to a 2010 estimate by Harvard University economist Jeffrey Miron, replacing marijuana prohibition with a system of taxation and regulation would result in around $17.4 billion per year in reduced government spending and increased tax revenues. Another researcher estimated that the revenue lost from our failure to tax the marijuana industry could be as high as $31 billion!

The Use of Medical Marijuana

Many patients and their doctors find marijuana a useful medicine as part of the treatment for AIDS, cancer, glaucoma, multiple sclerosis, and other ailments. Yet the federal government allows only four patients in the United States to use marijuana as a medicine, through a program now closed to new applicants. Federal laws treat all other patients currently using medical marijuana as criminals. Doctors are presently allowed to prescribe cocaine and morphine—but not marijuana.

Organizations that have endorsed medical access to marijuana include the American Public Health Association, AIDS Action Council, Leukemia & Lymphoma Society, American Academy of HIV Medicine, American Nurses Association, Lymphoma Foundation of America, National Association of People with AIDS, Epilepsy Foundation, the state medical associations of Maryland, California, and Rhode Island, and many others.

A few of the many editorial boards that have endorsed medical access to marijuana include the *Boston Globe, Chicago Tribune, Miami Herald, New York Times, Orange County Register, USA Today, Baltimore Sun*, and the *Los Angeles Times*.

Support for Legalization

Since 1996, a majority of voters in Alaska, Arizona, California, Colorado, the District of Columbia, Maine, Massachusetts, Michigan, Montana, Nevada, Oregon, and Washington State have voted in favor of ballot initiatives to remove criminal penalties for seriously ill people who possess and safely access medical marijuana. Similar legislation has passed through the state legislatures in Connecticut, Delaware, Hawaii, Illinois, Maryland, Minnesota, New Hampshire, New Jersey, New Mexico, New York, Rhode Island, and Vermont.

Numerous polls, including Pew [Research Center], Gallup, and CNN, have found that the majority of Americans now believe marijuana use should be legal for adults. Support for legal access to medical marijuana has been consistently strong (e.g., 85% support according to a Fox News poll in 2013).

Voters in four states—Alaska, Colorado, Oregon, and Washington—have enacted measures making marijuana legal for adults aged 21 and over and replacing the current policies with systems similar to that used to regulate alcohol. Alaska, Colorado, and Oregon's laws also allow adults to grow modest amounts of cannabis.

In Colorado, the first state where retail sales began for adult use, taking marijuana off the criminal market and regulating it has created many thousands of jobs and generated tens of thousands of dollars in revenue. More than 10,000 occupational licenses have been issued for jobs created directly by Colorado's marijuana industry. Colorado collected over $41.6 million in retail marijuana taxes in the first eight months of sales—from January to September 2014.

Fifteen additional states have removed the possibility of jail time for possession of modest amounts of marijuana for personal use under most circumstances. Fines may be issued (somewhat similarly to traffic tickets), but there is typically no arrest, incarceration, or criminal record. Those states are California, Connecticut, Maine, Maryland, Massachusetts, Minnesota, Mississippi, Missouri (goes into effect in 2017), Nebraska, Nevada, New York, North Carolina, Ohio, Oregon, Rhode Island, and Vermont.

In November 2014, District of Columbia voters overwhelmingly passed an initiative to legalize the limited possession and cultivation of marijuana by adults who are 21 or older. (The measure must undergo congressional review before taking effect.)

The Negative Effects of Prohibition

Decriminalization saves a tremendous amount in enforcement costs. California saved an estimated $857 million in 2006 alone.

A 2001 National Research Council study sponsored by the U.S. government found "little apparent relationship between

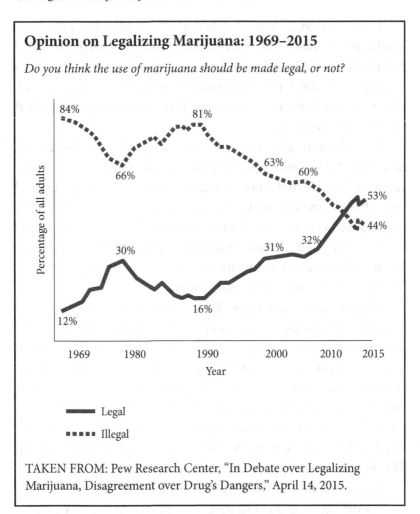

Opinion on Legalizing Marijuana: 1969–2015

Do you think the use of marijuana should be made legal, or not?

TAKEN FROM: Pew Research Center, "In Debate over Legalizing Marijuana, Disagreement over Drug's Dangers," April 14, 2015.

the severity of sanctions prescribed for drug use and prevalence or frequency of use, and . . . perceived legal risk explains very little in the variance of individual drug use." The primary evidence cited came from comparisons between states that have and have not decriminalized marijuana.

In the Netherlands, where adult possession and purchase of small amounts of marijuana are allowed under a regulated system, the rate of marijuana use by both teenagers and adults is lower than in the U.S., as is use of hard drugs such as cocaine. Under a regulated system, licensed merchants have an incentive to check IDs and avoid selling to minors. Such a system also separates marijuana from the trade in hard drugs such as cocaine and heroin.

"Zero tolerance" policies against "drugged driving" can result in "DUI" convictions of drivers who are not intoxicated at all. Trace amounts of THC [tetrahydrocannabinol, the main intoxicant in marijuana] metabolites detected by commonly used tests can linger in blood and urine for weeks after any psychoactive effects have worn off. This is equivalent to convicting someone of "drunk driving" weeks after he or she drank one beer.

The arbitrary criminalization of tens of millions of Americans who consume marijuana results in a large-scale lack of respect for the law and the entire criminal justice system.

Marijuana prohibition subjects users to added health hazards:

- Adulterants, contaminants, and impurities—Marijuana purchased through criminal markets is not subject to the same quality control standards as are legal consumer goods. Illicit marijuana may be adulterated with much more damaging substances; contaminated with pesticides, herbicides, or fertilizers; and/or infected with molds, fungi, or bacteria.

- Inhalation of hot smoke—One well-established hazard of marijuana consumption is the fact that smoke is bad for the respiratory system. Laws that prohibit the sale or possession of paraphernalia make it difficult to obtain and use vaporizers, which are proven to reduce these risks.

Because vigorous enforcement of marijuana laws forces the toughest, most dangerous criminals to take over marijuana trafficking, prohibition links marijuana sales to violence, predatory crime, and terrorism. According to the *Atlantic*, more than 50,000 people have lost their lives in Mexican drug cartel–related violence since 2006.

Prohibition invites corruption within the criminal justice system by giving officials easy, tempting opportunities to accept bribes, steal and sell marijuana, and plant evidence on innocent people.

Because marijuana is typically used in private, trampling the Bill of Rights is a routine part of marijuana law enforcement—e.g., use of drug dogs, urine tests, phone taps, government informants, curbside garbage searches, military helicopters, and infrared heat detectors.

> "Advocates are convinced that the mea-
> sures will survive any potential assaults
> on state sovereignty by the federal gov-
> ernment."

Two States Defy Feds with Full Marijuana Legalization

Alex Newman

*In the following viewpoint, Alex Newman argues that the legal-
ization of marijuana by Colorado and Washington State in 2012
(and later by Oregon and Alaska in 2014) will push the issue of
federal drug policy out in the open for a resolution. Newman
claims that although the federal government has taken charge of
drug policy, the latest changes in state policy illustrate why the
federal government should not be involved. Newman claims that
analysts believe the prohibition on all drugs will eventually come
to an end in the United States. Newman is a journalist.*

As you read, consider the following questions:

1. Marijuana was legalized in Colorado and Washington
   State by what percentage of voters, according to Newman?

Alex Newman, "Two States Defy Feds with Full Marijuana Legalization," Thenew
american.com, November 7, 2012. Copyright © 2012 The New American. All rights reserved. Reproduced with permission.

2. According to Newman, a coalition of what public figures opposes marijuana legalization and wants federal intervention?

3. According to Newman, what is the nullification movement, which he says the recent legalizations support?

Colorado and Washington became the first two states to nullify unconstitutional federal drug statutes by legalizing marijuana for recreational use, with voters backing Amendment 64 and Initiative 502—but rejecting a similar proposal in Oregon. The two victories for legalization advocates, however, have set the stage for a potential showdown with the Obama administration of historic importance.

In Colorado, about 55 percent of voters supported Amendment 64, which changes the state constitution to treat cannabis—already legal for medicinal purposes in the state—similar to alcohol and tobacco. Sales of marijuana will be regulated and taxed, with the increased revenue going to the state's general fund and toward building government schools. Local authorities, however, still have power to restrict or prohibit sales within their jurisdictions.

"Over the past eight years in Colorado, we have argued that it is irrational to punish adults for choosing to use a product that is far less harmful than alcohol," said codirector Mason Tvert with the pro–Amendment 64 Campaign to Regulate Marijuana Like Alcohol. "Today, the voters agreed. Colorado will no longer have laws that steer people toward using alcohol, and adults will be free to use marijuana instead if that is what they prefer. And we will be better off as a society because of it."

Initiative 502 in Washington State, meanwhile, was approved by around 55 percent of the electorate as well, legalizing the strictly regulated sale and consumption of marijuana for adults over the age of 21. The measure was tied to a new policy on "drugged driving," setting tight limits on the canna-bis content allowed in drivers' systems.

"I'm going to go ahead and give my victory speech right now. After this I can go sit down and stop shaking," said I-502 campaign manager Alison Holcomb. "Today the state of Washington looked at 75 years of national marijuana prohibition and said it is time for a new approach."

Separately, Massachusetts became the 18th state to nullify federal marijuana statutes by legalizing cannabis for medical purposes. Voters overwhelmingly supported the measure with 63 percent in favor, joining states across the country and Washington, D.C., in defying the feds as part of an effort to allow sick patients to legally consume the controversial plant as medicine. In Arkansas, voters rejected a similar proposal.

Analysts say the victories for nullification at the polls had much to do with the heavy support from certain law enforcement groups and medical experts, as well as recent moves by prominent conservative leaders to rally behind legalization. Polls show that since at least last year, most Americans now support legalizing marijuana despite fierce opposition from the drug-war "industry" and federal officials.

However, the federal government and its legions of drug warriors are not ready to give up the fight just yet. The Obama administration, which remained largely silent about the legal-ization initiatives throughout the campaign, has waged a ruth-less crackdown on medical marijuana even more vigorous than under the George W. Bush administration. And Depart-ment of Justice officials have hinted subtly that they may seek to quash the nullification victories in Colorado and Washing-ton.

Before the vote, a coalition of former White House drug czars and DEA [Drug Enforcement Administration] chiefs complained that Obama, who has admitted to consuming ille-gal drugs, had not vowed to unconstitutionally attempt to co-erce state governments into continuing prohibition. Among other points, the anti-legalization team warned that ending the costly war on marijuana would allegedly violate United Nations drug treaties.

The drug warriors also claimed that legalizing cannabis could even trigger a "constitutional showdown." However, they were apparently unaware that the U.S. Constitution does not delegate any power over drug policy to the federal government—that is why alcohol prohibition required a constitutional amendment.

Legal experts and pro-legalization activists believe voters in Washington and Colorado are standing on firm ground in their nullification efforts. With the wide array of law enforcement officials that lined up to support the measure, including U.S. attorney John McKay in Seattle under former president George W. Bush, advocates are convinced that the measures will survive any potential assaults on state sovereignty by the federal government.

"Our nation was founded upon the idea that states would be free to determine their own policies on matters not delegated to the federal government," Colorado legalization campaign codirector Tvert told the *Huffington Post*, noting that many of the opponents had made their living based on the unconstitutional prohibition policy. "We hope the Obama administration respects these state-based policy debates."

Colorado Gov. John Hickenlooper, a Democrat who opposed total legalization, also recognized the potential for a showdown with the federal government. However, he still vowed to uphold the will of the people while reminding voters that there could possibly be a drawn out battle before their wishes are fully implemented.

"The voters have spoken and we have to respect their will," the governor explained after the preliminary results were announced. "This will be a complicated process, but we intend to follow through. That said, federal law still says marijuana is an illegal drug, so don't break out the Cheetos or Goldfish too quickly."

Supporters of the U.S. Constitution, state sovereignty, and the Tenth Amendment celebrated the victory as yet another win for the growing nullification movement, which aims to restrict the federal government to its proper functions by nullifying unconstitutional statutes at the state level. However, across the board, proponents of legalization also emphasized that advocating an end to prohibition and unconstitutional federal policies should not be seen as an endorsement of marijuana use.

There were also critics who had other concerns. Numerous hard-core libertarians, for example, warned that the new regulatory and taxation regime over marijuana being erected in both Colorado and Washington State might be even more burdensome than the problems inherent in black markets. The plant could even end up being more expensive.

Some anti-marijuana activists worried that drug use among youth, which is already widespread, could increase. Others expressed concerns about how the measures will increase the cost and power of an already big state government, too.

"The initiative here in Washington, while good on the state sovereignty point, is bad in that it massively expands the size and scope of government paid for by a tax increase," liberty-minded Republican state Rep. Matthew Shea, who won reelection with more than 56 percent support, told the *New American* in an email.

Overall, though, the effects of the two measures will reverberate across the nation and probably even around the world. More than a few analysts celebrated the victories as the beginning of the end for the increasingly unpopular policy of prohibition, which has devoured over a trillion U.S. taxpayer dollars and countless lives around the world while enriching drug cartels and doing virtually nothing to reduce drug use.

"These victories likely represent the beginning of the end of marijuana prohibition in this country and many others as well," wrote executive director Ethan Nadelmann with the Drug Policy Alliance in a column for *USA Today*. "Just as the repeal of alcohol prohibition began in the late 1920s with individual states repealing their own prohibition laws, and ultimately culminated with repeal of federal prohibition, so Washington and Colorado have initiated a political process that will resonate nationally."

Whether the federal government tries to step in and quash the will of voters or not, analysts say it is only a matter of time before the drug war eventually comes to an end—especially considering the dire financial condition of the debt-laden U.S. government. In the meantime, though, Obama has vowed to continue waging and expanding the war around the world as part of his unconstitutional foreign policy of lawless interventionism. Of that, Americans can certainly expect at least four more years.

Periodical and Internet Sources Bibliography

The following articles have been selected to supplement the diverse views presented in this chapter.

Doug Bandow	"It's Time to Declare Peace in the War Against Drugs," *Forbes*, October 17, 2011.
Elizabeth Dickinson	"Legalizing Drugs Won't Stop Mexico's Brutal Cartels," *Foreign Policy*, June 22, 2011.
Drug Policy Alliance	"Just a Slap on the Wrist? The Life-Changing Consequences of a Marijuana Arrest," October 14, 2015.
Lee Fang	"The Real Reason Pot Is Still Illegal," *Nation*, July 2, 2014.
Doug Fine	"Marijuana Prohibition Hanging by a Thread," *Salon*, November 1, 2012.
Colin Flaherty	"Does Racism Really Cause More Black Drug Arrests?," *FrontPage Mag*, July 9, 2013.
Morgan Fox	"Stop Wasting Time Pretending Marijuana Prohibition Works," *U.S. News & World Report*, October 30, 2012.
Conor Friedersdorf	"Obama's Critique of Young People Who Want Legal Marijuana," *Atlantic*, March 17, 2015.
Anthony Gregory	"The Right & the Drug War," *American Conservative*, September 12, 2012.
Carl L. Hart	"Pot Reform's Race Problem," *Nation*, October 30, 2013.
John W. Whitehead	"America's Longest Ongoing War: The 'Race' War on Drugs," Rutherford Institute, January 9, 2012.

OPPOSING
VIEWPOINTS®
SERIES

Chapter 2

Is Marijuana
Use Harmful?

Chapter Preface

One of the key issues in the debate about marijuana legalization is the issue of harm. Many of the justifications for prohibition depend upon the accurateness of the claim that marijuana is harmful to the marijuana user, general society, or both. Even if marijuana were determined to be completely harmless, this would not eliminate all possible arguments in favor of prohibition; there are those who make the argument for the restriction on any mind-altering substances and call for laws that reflect that. Nonetheless, most people would agree that any valid argument in favor of prohibition must prove that the harms of marijuana are to such a degree that they outweigh the benefit of allowing people the freedom to use marijuana if they desire to do so.

One concern about marijuana legalization is its potential to harm the user. The concern about harm includes both short-term and long-term effects. One concern about short-term marijuana use is the risk of any immediate negative health reactions that may put the user's well-being at risk. Beyond the concern about acute effects, there is concern about the long-term effects of marijuana use, such as addiction. Proponents of marijuana legalization do not need to show that marijuana use has no harms to the user in order to make an argument consistent with the regulation of other substances. Society allows adults to consume alcohol and tobacco products, which are not free from both short-term and long-term harms. However, if the argument can be made that the harms of marijuana use are severe to the user, this may justify marijuana prohibition.

Another concern about marijuana legalization is its impact on society. If marijuana production and use result in unacceptable harmful effects on public safety, social order, or public health systems, prohibition may be justified. Again, though, marijuana use need not be completely harmless to society for a successful argument in favor of legalization. Regulation of legal marijuana akin to regulation of alcohol could avoid problems with underage use, drugged driving, or environmental degradation depending upon the severity of the social harms caused by marijuana production and use.

As the authors of the viewpoints in the following chapter illustrate, there exists widespread disagreement—even downright contradictory assessment—regarding the harmfulness of marijuana. Yet, without resolving this issue, it will be difficult to make a convincing case—one way or the other—regarding the ideal legal status of marijuana.

"Using marijuana causes impaired thinking and interferes with a user's ability to learn and to perform complicated tasks."

Marijuana Has Harmful Individual and Social Consequences

National Institute on Drug Abuse

In the following viewpoint, the National Institute on Drug Abuse (NIDA) argues that the chemical components of marijuana cause impairment of the brain, affecting memories, thinking, judgment, and coordination. NIDA claims that marijuana is addictive and that use of marijuana creates a gateway effect to other drug use. NIDA argues that marijuana use has negative effects on school, work, social life, and general physical health. NIDA is part of the National Institutes of Health of the US Department of Health and Human Services, providing national leadership for research on drug abuse and addiction.

As you read, consider the following questions:

1. What is the main psychoactive chemical in marijuana that causes most of the intoxicating effects, according to the author?

National Institute on Drug Abuse, "Marijuana," drugabuse.gov, April 2015, pp. 1, 3–8, 10–11. Courtesy of the National Institutes of Health (NIH).

2. What percentage of people who use marijuana will become dependent upon it, according to the viewpoint?

3. The author claims that after inhaling marijuana smoke one's heart rate may increase by how many beats per minute?

Marijuana—also called *weed, herb, pot, grass, bud, ganja, Mary Jane,* and a vast number of other slang terms—is a greenish-gray mixture of the dried, shredded leaves and flowers of *Cannabis sativa*—the hemp plant. Some users smoke marijuana in hand-rolled cigarettes called *joints*; many use pipes, water pipes (sometimes called *bongs*), or marijuana cigars called *blunts* (often made by slicing open cigars and replacing some or all of the tobacco with marijuana). Marijuana can also be used to brew tea and, particularly when it is sold or consumed for medicinal purposes, is frequently mixed into foods ("edibles") such as brownies, cookies, or candies. In addition, concentrated resins containing high doses of marijuana's active ingredients, including honey-like "hash oil," waxy "budder," and hard amber-like "shatter," are increasingly popular among both recreational and medical users.

The main *psychoactive* (mind-altering) chemical in marijuana, responsible for most of the intoxicating effects sought by recreational users, is delta-9-tetrahydrocannabinol (THC). The chemical is found in resin produced by the leaves and buds primarily of the female cannabis plant. The plant also contains more than 500 other chemicals, including over 100 compounds that are chemically related to THC, called *cannabinoids*. . . .

The Effects of Marijuana

When marijuana is smoked, THC and other chemicals in the plant pass from the lungs into the bloodstream, which rapidly carries them throughout the body and to the brain. The user begins to experience their effects almost immediately. Many users experience a pleasant euphoria and sense of relaxation. Other common effects, which may vary dramatically among different users, include heightened sensory perception (e.g., brighter colors), laughter, altered perception of time, and increased appetite.

If marijuana is consumed in foods or beverages, these effects are somewhat delayed—usually appearing after 30 minutes to 1 hour—because the drug must first pass through the digestive system. Eating or drinking marijuana delivers significantly less THC into the bloodstream than smoking an equivalent amount of the plant. Because of the delayed effects, users may inadvertently consume more THC than they intend to.

Pleasant experiences with marijuana are by no means universal. Instead of relaxation and euphoria, some users experience anxiety, fear, distrust, or panic. These effects are more common when too much is taken, the marijuana has an unexpectedly high potency, or a user is inexperienced. People who have taken large doses of marijuana may experience an acute psychosis, which includes hallucinations, delusions, and a loss of the sense of personal identity. These unpleasant but temporary reactions are distinct from longer-lasting psychotic disorders, such as schizophrenia, that may be associated with the use of marijuana in vulnerable individuals.

Although detectable amounts of THC may remain in the body for days or even weeks after use, the noticeable effects of smoked marijuana generally last from 1 to 3 hours and those of marijuana consumed in food or drink may last for many hours.

Impairment of the Brain

THC and other cannabinoid chemicals in marijuana are similar to cannabinoid chemicals that naturally occur in the body. These *endogenous cannabinoids* function as *neurotransmitters* because they send chemical messages between nerve cells (*neurons*) throughout the nervous system. They affect brain areas that influence pleasure, memory, thinking, concentration, movement, coordination, and sensory and time perception. Because of this similarity, THC is able to attach to molecules called *cannabinoid receptors* on neurons in these brain areas and activate them, disrupting various mental and physical functions and causing the effects described earlier. The neural communication network that uses these cannabinoid neurotransmitters, known as the *endocannabinoid system*, plays a critical role in the nervous system's normal functioning, so interfering with it can have profound effects.

For example, THC is able to alter the functioning of the hippocampus and orbitofrontal cortex, brain areas that enable a person to form new memories and shift their attentional focus. As a result, using marijuana causes impaired thinking and interferes with a user's ability to learn and to perform complicated tasks. THC also disrupts functioning of the cerebellum and basal ganglia, brain areas that regulate balance, posture, coordination, and reaction time. This is the reason people who have used marijuana may not be able to drive a car safely and may be impaired at playing sports or other physical activities.

THC, acting through cannabinoid receptors, also activates the brain's reward system, which includes regions that govern the response to healthy pleasurable behaviors like sex and eating. Like most other drugs of abuse, THC stimulates neurons in the reward system to release the signaling chemical *dopamine* at levels higher than typically observed in response to natural stimuli. This flood of dopamine contributes to the pleasurable "high" that recreational marijuana users seek.

Marijuana significantly impairs judgment, motor coordination, and reaction time, and studies have found a direct relationship between blood THC concentration and impaired driving ability. Marijuana is the illicit drug most frequently found in the blood of drivers who have been involved in accidents, including fatal ones (although it is important to note that marijuana can remain detectable in body fluids for days or even weeks after acute intoxication). A meta-analysis of multiple studies found that the risk of being involved in an accident roughly doubles after marijuana use.

Accident-involved drivers with THC in their blood, particularly higher levels, are three to seven times more likely to be responsible for the accident than drivers who had not used drugs or alcohol. The risk associated with marijuana in combination with alcohol appears to be greater than that for either drug by itself. . . .

The Addictiveness of Marijuana

Over time, overstimulation of the endocannabinoid system by marijuana use can cause changes in the brain that lead to *addiction*, a condition in which a person cannot stop using a drug even though it interferes with many aspects of his or her life. It is estimated that 9 percent of people who use marijuana will become dependent on it. The number goes up to about 17 percent in those who start using young (in their teens) and to 25 to 50 percent among daily users. According to the 2013 NSDUH [National Survey on Drug Use and Health], marijuana accounted for 4.2 million of the estimated 6.9 million Americans dependent on or abusing illicit drugs.

Marijuana addiction is linked to a mild withdrawal syndrome. Frequent marijuana users often report irritability, mood and sleep difficulties, decreased appetite, cravings, restlessness, and/or various forms of physical discomfort that peak within the first week after quitting and last up to 2 weeks.

Substantial evidence from animal research and a growing number of studies in humans indicate that marijuana exposure during development can cause long-term or possibly permanent adverse changes in the brain. Rats exposed to THC before birth, soon after birth, or during adolescence show notable problems with specific learning and memory tasks later in life. Cognitive impairments in adult rats exposed to THC during adolescence are associated with structural and functional changes in the hippocampus. Studies in rats also show that adolescent exposure to THC is associated with an altered reward system, increasing the likelihood that an animal will self-administer other drugs (e.g., heroin) when given an opportunity. Imaging studies in human adolescents show that regular marijuana users display impaired neural connectivity in specific brain regions involved in a broad range of executive functions like memory, learning, and impulse control compared to nonusers.

The latter findings may help explain the results of a large longitudinal study conducted in New Zealand, which found that frequent and persistent marijuana use starting in adolescence was associated with a loss of an average of 8 IQ [intelligence quotient] points measured in mid-adulthood. Significantly, in that study, those who used marijuana heavily as teenagers and quit using as adults did not recover the lost IQ points. Users who only began using marijuana heavily in adulthood did not lose IQ points. These results suggest that marijuana has its strongest long-term impact on young users whose brains are still busy building new connections and maturing in other ways. The endocannabinoid system is known to play an important role in the proper formation of synapses (the connections between neurons) during early brain development, and a similar role has been proposed for the refinement of neural connections during adolescence. If confirmed by future research, this may be one avenue by which marijuana use during adolescence produces its long-term effects.

The ability to draw definitive conclusions about marijuana's long-term impact on the human brain from past studies is often limited by the fact that study participants use multiple substances, and there is often limited data about the participants' health or mental functioning prior to the study. Over the next decade, the National Institutes of Health is planning to fund a major longitudinal study that will track a large sample of young Americans from late childhood (before first use of drugs) to early adulthood. The study will use neuroimaging and other advanced tools to clarify precisely how and to what extent marijuana and other substances, alone and in combination, affect adolescent brain development.

Marijuana's Gateway Effect

Is marijuana a gateway drug?

Early exposure to cannabinoids in adolescent rodents decreases the reactivity of brain dopamine reward centers later in adulthood. To the extent that these findings generalize to humans, this could help explain early marijuana initiates' increased vulnerability for drug abuse and addiction to other substances of abuse later in life that has been reported by most epidemiological studies. It is also consistent with animal experiments showing THC's ability to "prime" the brain for enhanced responses to other drugs. For example, rats previously administered THC show heightened behavioral response not only when further exposed to THC but also when exposed to other drugs such as morphine—a phenomenon called *cross-sensitization*.

These findings are consistent with the idea of marijuana as a "gateway drug." However, most people who use marijuana do not go on to use other, "harder" substances. Also, cross-sensitization is not unique to marijuana. Alcohol and nicotine also prime the brain for a heightened response to other drugs and are, like marijuana, also typically used before a person progresses to other, more harmful substances.

It is important to note that other factors besides biological mechanisms, such as a person's social environment, are also critical in a person's risk for drug use. An alternative to the gateway-drug hypothesis is that people who are more vulnerable to drug-taking are simply more likely to start with readily available substances like marijuana, tobacco, or alcohol, and their subsequent social interactions with other drug users increases their chances of trying other drugs. Further research is needed to explore this question.

The Negative Effects of Marijuana

Research has shown that marijuana's negative effects on attention, memory, and learning can last for days or weeks after the acute effects of the drug wear off, depending on the user's history with the drug. Consequently, someone who smokes marijuana daily may be functioning at a reduced intellectual level most or all of the time. Considerable evidence suggests that students who smoke marijuana have poorer educational outcomes than their nonsmoking peers. For example, a review of 48 relevant studies found marijuana use to be associated with reduced educational attainment (i.e., reduced chances of graduating). A recent analysis using data from three large studies in Australia and New Zealand found that adolescents who used marijuana regularly were significantly less likely than their non-using peers to finish high school or obtain a degree. They also had a much higher chance of later developing dependence, using other drugs, and attempting suicide. Several studies have also linked heavy marijuana use to lower income, greater welfare dependence, unemployment, criminal behavior, and lower life satisfaction.

To what degree marijuana use is directly causal in these associations remains an open question requiring further research. It is possible that other factors independently predispose people to both marijuana use and various negative life outcomes such as school dropout. That said, marijuana users themselves report a perceived influence of their marijuana use on poor outcomes on a variety of life satisfaction and achievement measures. One study, for example, compared current and former long-term, heavy users of marijuana with a control group who reported smoking marijuana at least once in their lives but not more than 50 times. All participants had similar education and income backgrounds, but significant differences were found in their educational attainment: Fewer of the heavy cannabis users completed college and more had yearly household incomes less than $30,000. When asked how marijuana affected their cognitive abilities, career achievements, social lives, and physical and mental health, the majority of heavy users reported that marijuana had negative effects in all these areas of their lives.

Studies have also suggested specific links between marijuana use and adverse consequences in the workplace, such as increased risk for injury or accidents. One study among postal workers found that employees who tested positive for marijuana on a pre-employment urine drug test had 55 percent more industrial accidents, 85 percent more injuries, and 75 percent greater absenteeism compared with those who tested negative for marijuana use. . . .

Within a few minutes after inhaling marijuana smoke, a person's heart rate speeds up, the breathing passages relax and become enlarged, and blood vessels in the eyes expand, making the eyes look bloodshot (red). The heart rate—normally 70 to 80 beats per minute—may increase by 20 to 50 beats per minute or may even double in some cases. Taking other drugs with marijuana can amplify this effect.

Limited evidence suggests that a person's risk of heart attack during the first hour after smoking marijuana is nearly five times his or her usual risk. This observation could be partly explained by marijuana raising blood pressure (in some cases) and heart rate and reducing the blood's capacity to carry oxygen. Marijuana may also cause *orthostatic hypotension* (head rush or dizziness on standing up), possibly raising danger from fainting and falls. Tolerance to some cardiovascular effects often develops with repeated exposure. These health effects need to be examined more closely, particularly given the increasing use of "medical marijuana" by people with health issues and older adults who may have increased baseline vulnerability due to age-related cardiovascular risk factors.

Marijuana smoke, like tobacco smoke, is an irritant to the throat and lungs and can cause a heavy cough during use. It also contains toxic gases and particles that can damage the lungs. Marijuana smoking is associated with large airway inflammation, increased airway resistance, and lung hyperinflation, and regular marijuana smokers report more symptoms of chronic bronchitis than nonsmokers. Smoking marijuana may also reduce the respiratory system's immune response, increasing the likelihood of the user acquiring respiratory infections, including pneumonia. One study found that frequent marijuana smokers used more sick days than other people, often because of respiratory illnesses.

Whether smoking marijuana causes lung cancer, as cigarette smoking does, is less certain. Although marijuana smoke contains *carcinogenic* (cancer-causing) combustion products, evidence for a link between marijuana use and lung cancer has thus far been inconclusive. The very different ways marijuana and tobacco are used, including factors like how frequently they are smoked during the day and how long the smoke is held in the lungs, as well as the fact that many people use both substances make determining marijuana's precise contribution to lung cancer risk, if any, difficult to establish. This is an area that will require more research.

However, a few studies have shown a clear link between marijuana use in adolescence and increased risk for an aggressive form of testicular cancer (nonseminomatous testicular germ cell tumor) that predominantly strikes young adult males. The early onset of testicular cancers compared to lung and most other cancers indicates that, whatever the nature of marijuana's contribution, it may accumulate over just a few years of use.

"Cannabinoids have a relatively unique safety record, particularly when compared to other therapeutically active substances."

Marijuana Has Been Used for Centuries and Is Relatively Safe

Paul Armentano

In the following viewpoint, Paul Armentano argues that marijuana has been cultivated and used by human beings for thousands of years as medicine, as a drug, as a fiber, and as food. Armentano claims that research shows the impact of cannabinoids varies and—although not completely harmless—overall the consumption of marijuana has a positive safety record. He contends that there are different methods for consuming marijuana, some of which may be safer than others. Armentano is the deputy director of the National Organization for the Reform of Marijuana Laws (NORML) and the NORML Foundation.

As you read, consider the following questions:

1. According to Armentano, what piece of legislation outlawed the recreational, industrial, and therapeutic use of marijuana?

Paul Armentano, "Marijuana: A Primer," Norml.org, January 29, 2013, pp. 1–6. Copyright © 2013 NORML. All rights reserved. Reproduced with permission.

2. What FDA-approved pharmaceutical product does the author say has been approved for medical use?

3. According to the author, in what three ways can marijuana be consumed by inhalation?

The term 'marijuana' (sometimes spelled 'marihuana') is Mexican in origin and typically refers to any part of—or any one of—the three distinctive subspecies of the cannabis plant: *cannabis sativa* (which tends to grow tall and stalky), *cannabis indica* (which tends to grow smaller and bushier), or *cannabis ruderalis* (found primarily in Russia and Eastern Europe). Grown outdoors, the cannabis plant typically achieves maturity within three to five months. Cultivated indoors under optimum heat and lighting, the plant may reach maturity within as few as 60 days.

The Historical Cultivation of Marijuana

Humans have cultivated and consumed the flowering tops of the female cannabis plant since virtually the beginning of recorded history. Cannabis-based textiles dating to 7,000 BC have been recovered in northern China, and the plant's use as a medicinal and euphoric agent date back nearly as far. In 2008, archeologists in central Asia discovered over two pounds of cannabis in the 2,700-year-old grave of an ancient mummified shaman. After scientists [Ethan B. Russo et al.] conducted extensive testing on the material's potency, they affirmed, "[T]he most probable conclusion . . . is that [ancient] culture[s] cultivated cannabis for pharmaceutical, psychoactive, and divinatory purposes."

Modern cultures continue to utilize cannabis for these same purposes, despite a present-day, nearly worldwide ban on the plant's cultivation and consumption imposed by various governments. In the United States, Congress initially imposed federal prohibitions outlawing cannabis's recreational, industrial, and therapeutic use by the passage of the Marihuana Tax Act of 1937. This federal prohibition was later reaffirmed by Congress' decision to classify marijuana—as well as all of the plant's active compounds, known as cannabinoids—as Schedule I substances under the Controlled Substances Act of 1970. This classification, which asserts by statute that cannabis is equally as dangerous to the public as heroin and is more dangerous than cocaine, defines cannabis and its dozens of distinct cannabinoids as possessing "a high potential for abuse . . . no currently accepted medical use, . . . [and] a lack of accepted safety for the use of the drug . . . under medical supervision." By contrast, cocaine and methamphetamine—which remain illicit for recreational use but are allowed as prescription drug agents—are classified as Schedule II drugs. Examples of Schedule III and IV substances include anabolic steroids and Valium, respectively, while the law defines codeine-containing cough suppressants as Schedule V drugs, the federal government's most lenient classification.

Despite the U.S. government's nearly century-long prohibition of the plant, scientists in America and around the world have continued to closely study the plant and its effects on living organisms, including in clinical trials. In recent years, scientists' interest in the plant and its active constituents, known as cannabinoids, has increased exponentially. Scientific study of the cannabis plant has now identified over 60 unique, biologically active cannabinoids . . . many of which possess documented therapeutic properties. A recent meta-analysis of these compounds identifies well over a dozen therapeutic properties attributable to cannabinoids, including neuroprotective, anti-cancer, anti-bacterial, and anti-diabetic properties. To date, there are over 22,000 published studies or reviews in the scientific literature pertaining to the cannabis plant and its cannabinoids. Nearly one-half of these were published within the last five years. This total includes over 2,700 separate papers published in 2009, 1,950 papers published in 2010, another 2,450 published in 2011, and over 2,900 papers published in 2012, according to a key word search on PubMed, the U.S. government repository for peer-reviewed scientific research. . . .

The Uses of Cannabis

Historically, humans have used various parts of the cannabis plant for a multitude of purposes. Most people today are readily aware that cannabis is consumed socially as a mood enhancer. By contrast, certain varieties of cannabis—as well as most parts of the plant, including the seeds and the stalk—contain virtually no psychoactive properties but may be utilized in other ways. For example, ground seeds from the cannabis plant contain high and balanced levels of essential amino acids and essential fatty acids and may be baked into a variety of nutritional foodstuffs, such as bread, butter, and salad dressing. Oil can also be processed from cannabis seeds and used for sautéing or consumed as a nutritional supplement. Since the seeds contain negligible amounts of the plant's primary psychoactive agent, the importation and domestic sale of certain cannabis-based foods, oils, and sterilized seeds is permitted in the United States under federal law.

The stalk of the marijuana plant, primarily of the *cannabis sativa* variety—which can grow as high as 20 feet in height—can also be harvested for bast fiber content. This renewable resource is a common source of paper, rope, and clothing. Most industrialized nations, including Canada, Japan, Australia, and the European Union, regulate the commercial production of low THC [tetrahydrocannabinol, the chief intoxicant in marijuana] varieties of cannabis for industrial purposes. During World War II, the U.S. government commissioned tens of thousands of domestic farmers to grow cannabis to assist with America's wartime needs. Following the war's conclusion, however, the United States' government imposed a complete ban on the domestic production of the plant, including the cultivation of non-psychoactive *cannabis sativa* varieties. That ban continues today.

The plant's cannabinoids are largely responsible for cannabis's physiological, mood-altering, and therapeutic effects. THC, the most studied of all the plant's cannabinoids, is psychoactive and is primarily responsible for the plant's influence on mood and behavior. It also possesses various therapeutic effects. Most acknowledged among these are pain relief, appetite stimulation, nausea and vomiting mitigation, anti-spasticity and anti-spasmodic effects, and intraocular pressure reduction in patients with glaucoma. An isolated stereoisomer of THC is presently available as the FDA [Food and Drug Administration]–approved product dronabinol, which is classified under federal law as a Schedule III substance. It is FDA approved as an appetite stimulant and as an anti-emetic in patients with HIV/AIDS or undergoing chemotherapy treatment. A number of additional, non-psychotropic cannabinoids such as CBD [cannabidiol] also possess numerous therapeutic properties. . . .

The Impact of Cannabinoids on the Body

Subjects experience psychological and physiological effects after ingesting cannabis because cannabinoids, THC in particular, interact with a complex and dense receptor system within the body. The CB1 [cannabinoid receptor type 1] receptors, first identified in the late 1980s, reside predominantly in the nervous system and their stimulation is responsible for the plant's psychoactive and behavioral effects, among other functions. The CB2 [cannabinoid receptor type 2] receptors, identified in the early 1990s, reside primarily in the immune system and are involved in the moderation of a number of biological functions, including inflammation and pain response. Naturally occurring chemicals in the human body (so-called endocannabinoids), which possess a similar molecular structure to herbal cannabinoids, act as neuromodulators and cytokine modulators within this receptor system to regulate many of the body's essential physiological functions—including appetite, blood pressure, reproduction, bone growth, tumor modulation, immunity, inflammation, pain sensation, memory, and muscle tone, among others. It is theorized that a properly functioning endogenous cannabinoid receptor system is necessary for good health and that certain disease types may be the result of deficiencies within this system. According to a National Institutes of Health review, "[M]odulating the activity of the endocannabinoid system ... hold[s] therapeutic promise in a wide range of disparate diseases and pathological conditions, ranging from mood and anxiety disorders, movement disorders such as Parkinson's and Huntington's disease, neuropathic pain, multiple sclerosis and spinal cord injury, to cancer, atherosclerosis, myocardial infarction, stroke, hypertension, glaucoma, obesity/metabolic syndrome, and osteoporosis, to name just a few." ...

What are some of the specific psychological and physical effects subjects will experience after consuming cannabis? The answer to this question often varies from subject to subject. Many of the plant's effects are dependent on percentage of THC and other cannabinoids present in the cannabis consumed. (The cannabinoid CBD, for instance, counteracts some of the psychoactivity of THC.) Moreover, cannabis-naive users tend to experience different effects compared to more experienced users who have become tolerant to some of the cannabinoids' mood-altering and physiological qualities. If a less experienced user consumes too much cannabis at one time, he or she may experience a mix of unpleasant physical and psychological feelings, such as a tachycardia (rapid heartbeat), dry mouth, and a growing sense of paranoia. (These adverse effects are commonly referred to as a 'panic

Marijuana for Pain

For many seriously ill people, medical marijuana is the only medicine that relieves their pain and suffering, or treats symptoms of their medical condition, without debilitating side effects. Marijuana's medicinal benefits are incontrovertible, now proven by decades of peer-reviewed, controlled studies published in highly respected medical journals. Marijuana has been shown to alleviate symptoms of a wide range of debilitating medical conditions including cancer, HIV/AIDS, multiple sclerosis, alzheimer's disease, post-traumatic stress disorder (PTSD), epilepsy, Crohn's disease, and glaucoma, and is often an effective alternative to narcotic painkillers.

Evidence of marijuana's efficacy in treating severe and intractable pain is particularly impressive. Researchers at the University of California conducted a decade of randomized, double-blind, placebo-controlled clinical trials on the medical utility of inhaled marijuana, concluding that marijuana should be a "first line treatment" for patients with painful neuropathy, who often do not respond to other available treatments.

Drug Policy Alliance,
"Marijuana: The Facts."

attack.') These feelings, while mildly unpleasant, are only temporary and pose little to no actual long-term risk to the user's health.

As cannabis consumers become more experienced with cannabis, they become more tolerant to some of the drug's physical effects. More experienced consumers also learn to better self-regulate (or 'titrate') their dosage to better avoid potentially dysphoric symptoms such as anxiety or paranoia.

The Safety Profile of Cannabis

Cannabinoids have a relatively unique safety record, particularly when compared to other therapeutically active substances. Most significantly, the consumption of cannabinoids—regardless of quantity or potency—cannot induce a fatal overdose because, unlike alcohol or opiates, they do not act as central nervous system depressants. According to a 1995 review prepared for the World Health Organization, "There are no recorded cases of overdose fatalities attributed to cannabis, and the estimated lethal dose for humans extrapolated from animal studies is so high that it cannot be achieved by . . . users."

Cannabinoids also appear to be largely nontoxic to healthy cells and organs. Writes Dr. Mitch Earleywine in the 2002 Oxford University Press publication *Understanding Marijuana: A New Look at the Scientific Evidence*, "[C]annabis is essentially non-toxic." A systematic review of clinical trials over a 40-year period, published in the *Canadian Medical Association Journal*, found no higher incidence of serious adverse effects from cannabis-consuming subjects compared to controls, and cited 'dizziness' as the primary reported non-serious adverse event reported.

Additionally, in some initial trials, cannabinoids have demonstrated neuroprotective properties against toxic agents and have shown profound anti-cancer properties. Stated the National Academy of Sciences, Institute of Medicine in its 1999 review, *Marijuana and Medicine: Assessing the Science Base*, "Except for the harms associated with smoking, the adverse effects of marijuana use are within the range of effects tolerated for other medications." A more recent meta-analysis [by Leslie Iversen] assessing the effects of long-term exposure to cannabis concludes, "Overall, by comparison with other drugs used mainly for 'recreational' purposes, cannabis could be rated to be a relatively safe drug."

Nonetheless, cannabis should not necessarily be viewed as a 'harmless' substance. Consuming cannabis will alter mood, influence emotions, and temporarily alter perception, so consumers are best advised to pay particular attention to their set (emotional state) and setting (environment) prior to using it. It should not be consumed immediately prior to driving or prior to engaging in tasks that require certain learning skills, such as the retention of new information. Further, there may be some populations that are susceptible to increased risks from the use of cannabis, such as adolescents, pregnant or nursing mothers, and patients with or who have a family history of mental illness. Patients with hepatitis C, decreased lung function (such as chronic obstructive pulmonary disease), or who have a history of heart disease or stroke may also be at a greater risk of experiencing certain adverse side effects from cannabis. As with any therapy, patients concerned about such risks should consult thoroughly with their physician before deciding whether the medical use of cannabis is safe and appropriate for them.

The Consumption of Marijuana

Cannabis is most often inhaled—either through a cigarette (joint), pipe, water pipe (also known colloquially as a 'bong'), or vaporizer. Consumers tend to prefer inhalation as a route of administration because they begin to experience cannabis's effects almost immediately after inhalation. This outcome allows them to moderate their dose as needed or in accordance with their particular preference, as well as to achieve immediate relief from pain, nausea, and other symptoms.

Regardless of whether a person is inhaling cannabis via a joint, pipe, or water pipe, they are still subjecting their lungs to potentially noxious smoke. However, studies have, to date, failed to link cannabis inhalation—even over the long term—to the sort of adverse pulmonary effects associated with tobacco smoking. According to a 2012 study [by Mark J. Pletcher et al.] published in the *Journal of the American Medical Association* (*JAMA*), lifetime, moderate cannabis smoking (defined as at least one joint per day for seven years or one joint per week for 49 years) was not associated with adverse effects on pulmonary function. Cannabis inhalation is also not associated with increased prevalence of certain types of cancers, such as melanoma, prostate cancer, or breast cancer. Nor has its use been associated with higher prevalence of tobacco-related cancers such as lung cancer. In 2006, the results of the largest case-controlled study ever to investigate the respiratory effects of marijuana smoking reported that cannabis use was not associated with lung-related cancers, even among subjects who reported smoking more than 22,000 joints over their lifetime. "We hypothesized that there would be a positive association between marijuana use and lung cancer, and that the association would be more positive with heavier use," one of the study's primary researchers, Dr. Donald Tashkin of the University of California at Los Angeles, stated. "What we found instead was no association at all, and even a suggestion of some protective effect."

The use of a water-pipe filtration system primarily cools cannabis smoke. However, this technology is not particularly efficient at eliminating the toxic by-products of combustion. As a result, some cannabis consumers utilize vaporizers, which heat marijuana to a point where cannabinoid vapors form, but below the point of combustion. This technology allows consumers to experience the rapid onset of the plant's effects while avoiding many of the associated respiratory hazards associated with smoking—such as coughing, wheezing, or chronic bronchitis. . . .

Consuming moderate to high quantities of marijuana orally, such as in food or in a tincture (a liquid-based solution), will yield a different and sometimes more intense outcome. Consumers will typically not begin to feel any psychoactive or physiological effects of the plant for at least 45 minutes to 90 minutes after ingestion. This delayed onset makes it more difficult for subjects to regulate their dosage.

Orally consumed cannabinoids tend to be stronger acting and last far longer (upwards of four to six hours is typical) than the effects of inhaled cannabis. This result is largely because of the way bodies metabolize THC. When cannabis is inhaled, THC passes rapidly from the lungs to the blood stream and to the brain. By contrast, when cannabis is consumed orally, a significant portion of THC is converted into the metabolite 11-hydroxy-THC before reaching the brain. (Inhaling cannabis produces only trace levels of this chemical.) Since this metabolite is believed to be slightly more potent than THC and possesses a greater blood-brain penetrability, the physical and psychoactive effects of the substance may be magnified in some consumers.

Some users prefer these longer-lasting effects, particularly those seeking to treat chronic conditions. Other consumers, such as those seeking occasional symptomatic relief or those less experienced to cannabis's effects, prefer the milder, shorter-lived effects associated with inhalation.

"Alcohol use is more damaging to the body than marijuana."

Research Shows That Marijuana Use Is Safer than Alcohol Use

Marijuana Policy Project

In the following viewpoint, the Marijuana Policy Project (MPP) argues that research indicates that the relative harm of marijuana when compared to alcohol is quite favorable. MPP claims that research shows marijuana is less addictive than alcohol and less damaging to the body. In addition, the author claims that studies indicate marijuana use does not cause the same harms to society as alcohol use, such as intoxication-related violence, sexual assault, and reckless behavior. MPP is an organization that aims to change laws to eliminate prohibition of medical and nonmedical use of marijuana.

As you read, consider the following questions:

1. According to the author, which US public figure noted that raw potatoes are more toxic than marijuana?

Marijuana Policy Project, "Marijuana Is Safer than Alcohol: It's Time to Treat It That Way," Mpp.org. Copyright © Marijuana Policy Project. All rights reserved. Reproduced with permission.

2. The author cites the US Centers for Disease Control and Prevention (CDC) as reporting how many annual US deaths attributed to alcohol use?

3. How many alcohol-related violent crimes does the US Department of Justice say occur annually, according to the author?

In 2008, research on marijuana's risk to health commissioned by nonpartisan British think tank the Beckley Foundation found: "The public health impact of contemporary patterns of cannabis use are modest by comparison with those of other illicit drugs (such as the opioids) or with alcohol. In the former case this reflects the absence of fatal overdose risk from cannabis. In the latter case, it reflects the much lower risks of death from cannabis than alcohol-impaired driving, fewer adverse effects on health, . . . and the lower rate of persistence of cannabis use into older adulthood."

The Relative Harm of Marijuana

In 2007, a team of experts was formed to conduct an analysis on the relative harms of marijuana, alcohol, and other drugs for the esteemed British medical journal the *Lancet*. It concluded that marijuana posed far fewer health and safety risks than alcohol. That same year, research commissioned by the Australian Institute of Health and Welfare arrived at the same conclusion. Specifically, it determined that alcohol was a significant contributor to death and responsible for 3.2% of the total burden of disease and injury in Australia, whereas marijuana was responsible for zero deaths and just 0.2% of the total burden of disease and injury.

In 2005, a University of Oxford meta-analysis [by Leslie Iversen] on marijuana concluded that even long-term marijuana use does not cause "any lasting physical or mental harm. . . . Overall, by comparison with other drugs used mainly for 'recreational' purposes, cannabis could be rated to be a relatively safe drug."

In 2002, an exhaustive review of marijuana and health performed by a special Canadian Senate committee found that "scientific evidence overwhelmingly indicates that cannabis is substantially less harmful than alcohol and should be treated not as a criminal issue but as a social and public health issue."

In the mid-1990s, the World Health Organization commissioned a study [by Wayne Hall] on the health and societal consequences of marijuana compared to alcohol, nicotine, and opiates. It concluded: "Overall, most of these risks [associated with marijuana] are small to moderate in size. In aggregate, they are unlikely to produce public health problems comparable in scale to those currently produced by alcohol and tobacco. . . . On existing patterns of use, cannabis poses a much less serious public health problem than is currently posed by alcohol and tobacco in Western societies."

On September 6, 1988, after hearing two years of testimony, Drug Enforcement Administration (DEA) chief administrative law judge Francis Young ruled: "In strict medical terms, marijuana is far safer than many foods we commonly consume. For example, eating 10 raw potatoes can result in a toxic response. By comparison, it is physically impossible to eat enough marijuana to induce death. Marijuana, in its natural form, is one of the safest therapeutically active substances known to man."

The Impact on the Consumer

Alcohol is more addictive than marijuana. According to a 1998 report by Drs. Jack E. Henningfield of the National Institute on Drug Abuse (NIDA) and Neal L. Benowitz of the University of California at San Francisco, alcohol's addiction potential is significantly greater than that of marijuana based on a number of indicators. A comprehensive federal study conducted by the National Academy of Sciences, Institute of Medicine [IOM] arrived at a similar conclusion: "Millions of Americans have tried marijuana, but most are not regular users [and] few marijuana users become dependent on it. . . . [A]lthough [some] marijuana users develop dependence, they appear to be less likely to do so than users of other drugs (including alcohol and nicotine), and marijuana dependence appears to be less severe than dependence on other drugs."

According to the IOM report, 15% of alcohol users ever meet the clinical criteria for a diagnosis of marijuana "dependence" based on the *Diagnostic and Statistical Manual of Mental Disorders* ([DSM] 3rd edition, revised), compared to 9% of marijuana users. Some experts believe significantly fewer than 9% of marijuana users are actually dependent because the DSM considers moderate, non-problematic marijuana use a "mental disorder," but goes out of its way to make the case that the moderate use of alcohol is not a disorder.

Alcohol use is more damaging to the body than marijuana. The health-related costs associated with alcohol use far exceed those for marijuana use. Health-related costs for alcohol consumers are eight times greater than those for marijuana consumers, according to an assessment published in British Columbia's *[Visions: BC's] Mental Health and Addictions Journal*. More specifically, the annual cost of alcohol consumption is $165 per user, compared to just $20 per user for marijuana. According to a 2006 report . . . alcohol is one of the most toxic drugs and using just 10 times the amount one would use to get the desired effect could lead to death. Marijuana is one of the least toxic drugs, with a fatal overdose near impossible.

The U.S. Centers for Disease Control and Prevention (CDC) reports that more than 37,000 annual U.S. deaths are attributed to the health effects of alcohol use, including hundreds of alcohol overdose deaths. The CDC does not have a category for deaths caused by marijuana use, and a

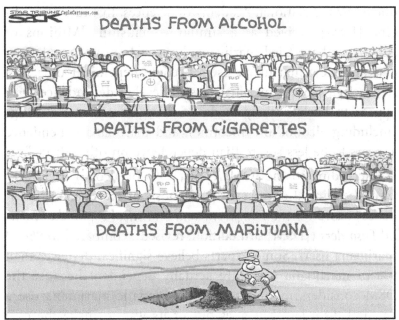

DEATHS FROM ALCOHOL

DEATHS FROM CIGARETTES

DEATHS FROM MARIJUANA

© Copyright 2014 Steve Sack. All Rights Reserved.

government-funded study conducted by researchers at Kaiser Permanente and published in the *American Journal of Public Health* found no association between marijuana use and premature death in otherwise healthy people.

Whereas alcohol use is associated with a wide variety of cancers, including cancers of the esophagus, stomach, colon, lungs, pancreas, liver and prostate, marijuana use has not been conclusively associated with any form of cancer. According to the U.S. National Academy of Sciences, Institute of Medicine, "There is no conclusive evidence that marijuana causes cancer in humans, including cancers usually related to tobacco use." This was reaffirmed in 2006 by the largest case-controlled study on the respiratory effects of marijuana smoking which, found "no association at all" between marijuana smoking and an increased risk of developing lung cancer, even among subjects who reported smoking more than 22,000 joints over their lifetimes.

The Impact on Society

Alcohol is more likely to contribute to acts of violence than marijuana. According to research [by Peter N.S. Hoaken and Sherry H. Stewart] published in the journal *Addictive Behaviors*, "Alcohol is clearly the drug with the most evidence to support a direct intoxication-violence relationship," whereas, "cannabis reduces the likelihood of violence during intoxication."

The U.S. Department of Health and Human Services estimates that 25% to 30% of violent crimes and 3% to 4% of property crimes in the U.S. are linked to the use of alcohol. According to a report from the U.S. Department of Justice, that translates to nearly 5,000,000 alcohol-related violent crimes per year. By contrast, the government does not even track violent acts specifically related to marijuana use, as the use of marijuana has not been associated with violence.

Alcohol is a particularly significant factor in the prevalence of domestic violence and sexual assault, whereas marijuana is not. This is not to say that alcohol causes these problems; rather, its use makes it more likely that an individual prone to such behavior will act on it. For example, investigators [W. Fals-Stewart, J. Golden, and J.A. Schumacher] at the Research Institute on Addictions reported, "The use of alcohol ... was associated with significant increases in the daily likelihood of male-to-female physical aggression," whereas the use of marijuana was "not significantly associated with an increased likelihood of male partner violence." Specifically, the odds of abuse were eight times higher on days when men were drinking; the odds of severe abuse were 11 times higher. The Rape, Abuse and Incest National Network's (RAINN) webpage dedicated to educating the public about "Drug Facilitated Sexual Assault" highlights alcohol as the "most commonly used chemical in crimes of sexual assault" and provides information on an array of other drugs that have been linked to sexual violence. The word "marijuana" does not appear anywhere on the page.

Alcohol is more likely to contribute to reckless behavior than marijuana. Research published in 2011 in the journal *Alcoholism: Clinical & Experimental Research*, concluded that an estimated 36% of hospitalized assaults and 21% of all injuries are attributable to alcohol use by the injured person. Meanwhile, the *American Journal of Emergency Medicine* reported that lifetime use of marijuana is rarely associated with emergency room visits. According to the British Advisory Council on the Misuse of Drugs: "Cannabis differs from alcohol . . . in one major respect. It does not seem to increase risk-taking behavior."

| "A society thrives when there are fewer
| drugs, not more."

Marijuana Use and Alcohol Use Are Dangerous for Society

Sven-Olov Carlsson

In the following viewpoint, Sven-Olov Carlsson, in a letter to President Barack Obama, argues that the claim that marijuana use is like alcohol use supports continued prohibition, not legalization. Carlsson claims that alcohol causes numerous harms to society as a legal drug and the fact that marijuana is like alcohol means that further harms through legalization ought to be avoided. Carlsson is president of IOGT International, a politically independent organization that advocates for a world free of alcohol and other drugs, and he is the international president of the World Federation Against Drugs.

As you read, consider the following questions:

1. According to the author, IOGT International operates in how many countries worldwide?

2. Carlsson contends that a report by a US government agency shows alcohol is responsible for how many million years of life lost in the United States each year?

Sven-Olov Carlsson, "Open Letter to President Barack Obama: The Notorious Comparison of Alcohol and Marijuana, and the Most Important Aspect That Is Conspicuously Absent," Iogt.org, January 29, 2014, pp. 1–3. Copyright © 2014 IOGT International. All rights reserved. Reproduced with permission.

3. The author claims that alcohol and what other drug are among the largest causes of ill health in the world?

Dear President [Barack] Obama,

It is with great interest that I have read your recent interview with David Remnick of the *New Yorker*. This article has initialed a myriad of emails and messages from IOGT International members from the USA and around the world reacting to your statements on alcohol and marijuana. As a result, I feel compelled to write to you to address the following as a matter of urgency.

IOGT International was founded more than 160 years ago, in 1851 in Utica, New York, in the USA. We are a global movement with more than 120 member organizations in more than 60 countries around the world. Through the work of all these members (the vast majority of them volunteers), we undertake prevention, treatment, rehabilitation and advocacy work to control and reduce the harms caused by alcohol and other drugs. It is no exaggeration to say that we are heart-driven experts in this field.

In the *New Yorker* article you state clearly that you "don't think [marijuana] is more dangerous than alcohol."

You follow that by saying using marijuana "is not something I encourage, and I've told my daughters I think it's a bad idea, a waste of time, [and] not very healthy."

Three Points

As you surely anticipated, the media jumped on these statements, exploiting your puzzling and contradictory messages about the legalization of marijuana and the comparison to alcohol. Headlines, articles and news pieces were largely omitting your critical remarks and concerns about marijuana legalization. These statements are deeply troubling. Please allow us, Mr. President, to explain why, in three concise points.

1) I believe you agree with the basic assumption that what is good for your daughters, Malia and Sasha, is good for all other children, too. All children in the USA have the right to grow up drug free. From this fundamental and heart-driven assumption follows that all children have a right to grow up free from drugs and associated harm. The Convention on the Rights of the Child (CRC) calls that "the right of every child to a standard of living adequate for the child's physical, mental, spiritual, moral and social development."

With this in mind, I would have wished for a much clearer statement that could not be misused by the legalization advocates, as has happened in the wake of your interview in the *New Yorker*. The members of IOGT International and many people around the world would have wished for a clear and concise commitment to making sure that the best interest principle enshrined in the CRC is held high: "In all actions concerning children, whether undertaken by public or private social welfare institutions, courts of law, administrative authorities or legislative bodies, the best interests of the child shall be a primary consideration."

I'm sure this is what you do as a father, and when it comes to harmful substances in society, I encourage you to also do this as the president of the USA.

2) To address the issue of marijuana in the way you did, by using the notorious comparison to alcohol, is indeed very dangerous. There are two reasons for this: Firstly, marijuana is highly dangerous, especially for the brain, for the mental health and well-being of the user but also for the community around the user and for society at large; you ran for president twice carried by a strong grassroots movement of active, engaged citizens. Marijuana is evidently a huge obstacle for active participation in society. And secondly, we live in an alcohol culture that glamorizes alcohol and perpetuates myths about its effects; people are not even aware of all the health

hazards and risks associated with alcohol, nor are they aware of all the damage to society, economy, community and the health system.

This adds up to a toxic mix of misinformation, perpetuated myths and the general assumption that it could be possible to regulate marijuana in the same way as alcohol. It is in this context that I think your quotes in the *New Yorker* are harmful because the fact is that the USA is failing in regulating alcohol and preventing alcohol harm. It is also failing in protecting children and young people from alcohol harm.

3) Alcohol is the socially most harmful drug. It is a toxic, teratogen and carcinogenic substance that causes tremendous harm to individuals, families, communities and society at large, because it's aggressively marketed, easily available and comparatively affordable. Alcohol is so harmful because we live in an intoxicating culture where it is available and affordable almost at any time, at any place and to anyone. Additionally it is aggressively being marketed to children and young people and other vulnerable groups.

Mr. President, it is this aspect that gets lost when comparing marijuana to alcohol: A society thrives when there are fewer drugs, not more. The most fundamental task of any government is to protect its citizens from harm, especially the most vulnerable ones. Thus, it should be your task to make sure there is less alcohol use in the USA, instead of blowing wind under the wings of the marijuana (and other drugs) legalization advocates. It is thanks to the international conventions on drugs and the CRC that marijuana is a lesser burden on society in terms of harm. Mr. President, this surely means we should *not* conduct experiments with human lives by legalizing more drugs. And we have to find ways to regulate alcohol more cost-effectively and with higher impact measures because the current policies are failing.

The Harms of Marijuana Once Legal

We must be careful drawing conclusions from past research on marijuana's effects for several reasons. First, alcohol and tobacco are linked to more morbidity and mortality in our society than other drugs, in part due to their widespread availability as legal substances.... Another reason we must be careful drawing conclusions from past research on marijuana's effects is the dramatic increase in concentrations of the marijuana plant's main psychoactive ingredient, tetrahydrocannabinol (THC) seen over the past couple decades, along with the new ways of administering high THC content (e.g., electronic cigarette devices). The potency of an average marijuana cigarette has steadily increased from roughly 3 percent THC in the early 1990s to 12.5 percent THC in 2013. During this same period, the potency of marijuana extracts (also known as "hash oil") has also climbed to what are now staggering levels: The average marijuana extract contains over 50 percent THC, with some samples containing more than 80 percent THC. This means some historical findings about health and developmental effects from marijuana use may not be relevant when trying to predict effects on contemporary users.

Nora D. Volkow, "Mixed Signals: The Administration's Policy on Marijuana, Part Four—Scientific Focus on the Adverse Health Effects of Marijuana Use," Testimony before the House Committee on Oversight and Government Reform, June 20, 2014.

The Harms of Alcohol

The Centers for Disease Control and Prevention (CDC) just released evidence that alcohol harm is directly responsible for about 88,000 deaths and 2.5 million years of potential life lost in the United States each year. This amounts to a staggering burden on the US economy of $223.5 billion.

Alcohol harm in the USA poses a disproportionate burden on young Americans.

Mr. President, consider the youngest and most vulnerable ones: There are 7.5 million children under the age of 18 living with at least one alcohol addicted parent. In America, fathers convicted of child abuse are 10 times more likely to be alcoholics.

The alcohol industry plays its unethical role, too. Just recently researchers of CAMY (the Center on Alcohol Marketing and Youth) have found evidence that the alcohol industry is using advertising to directly target underage viewers aged 18 to 20.

Alcohol is a major risk factor for noncommunicable diseases, including mental health problems and disorders. As was recently shown for college students, alcohol use exacerbates students' post-traumatic stress disorder and those students with post-traumatic stress disorder are likely to use more alcohol than their peers without the psychological condition. It creates a vicious circle really.

Mr. President, I congratulate you for your latest effort to tackle the epidemic of gender-based violence, including rape and sexual assault, on American university campuses. Anyone who spends some time at university and college campuses understands that this problem will not be solved without addressing alcohol.

We know that the costs of intimate partner violence in the USA exceed $8.3 billion yearly. In more than 55% of the cases, the perpetrators had consumed alcohol.

The Comparison

Just looking at this snapshot, it is clear that the USA has an alcohol problem—an alcohol problem burdening the youngest and the most vulnerable; an alcohol problem putting tremendous pressures on the health care system; an alcohol problem undermining the economy; an alcohol problem threatening the future of so many women and girls, of entire families and communities.

Comparing alcohol and marijuana in the way you did and in the way it can be picked up by marijuana (and other drugs) legalization advocates for their purposes is dangerous because it fails to take into account the human rights, for instance those of our children, and it misses the most fundamental questions that the entire debate should be about.

Alcohol, together with tobacco, is among the largest causes of ill health in the world, while at the same time this is preventable with the right kind of policies. It is a mistake of gigantic dimensions to legalize one more drug, marijuana, which will lead to an increase in use and damages at levels beyond control.

We think the issue of drug and alcohol policy will be a big part of your legacy as president, potentially undermining your goals of building a sustainable health care system, of putting the economy on track toward sustainability and of giving every young American a fair shot at the American dream.

"Legalization of marijuana would in-crease demand for the drug and almost certainly exacerbate drug-related crime."

Marijuana Trafficking and Use Are Linked with Crime

Charles D. Stimson

In the following viewpoint, Charles D. Stimson argues that not only is marijuana trafficking associated with crime, but also marijuana use itself is correlated with crime. Legalization of marijuana for recreational use in the Netherlands and for medi-cal use in California illustrates why legalization would lead to problems for neighborhoods and communities due to the nega-tive effects associated with legal use. Stimson is a senior legal fel-low at the Heritage Foundation and manager of the foundation's National Security Law Program in the Davis Institute for Inter-national Studies.

As you read, consider the following questions:

1. According to Stimson, what percentage of arrestees in the United States, England, and Australia test positive for marijuana?

Charles D. Stimson, "Legalizing Marijuana: Why Citizens Should Just Say No," Heritage.org, no. 56, September 13, 2010, pp. 5–7. Copyright © 2010 The Heritage Foundation. All rights reserved. Reproduced with permission.

2. By what factor has Los Angeles experienced an increase in robberies in areas surrounding cannabis clubs, according to the author?

3. Stimson cites a study by the RAND Corporation finding that legalization of marijuana could cause the price of the drug to fall by as much as what percentage?

Today, marijuana trafficking is linked to a variety of crimes, from assault and murder to money laundering and smuggling. Legalization of marijuana would increase demand for the drug and almost certainly exacerbate drug-related crime, as well as cause a myriad of unintended but predictable consequences.

Marijuana and Crime

To begin with, an astonishingly high percentage of criminals are marijuana users. According to a study by the RAND Corporation, approximately 60 percent of arrestees test positive for marijuana use in the United States, England, and Australia. Further, marijuana metabolites are found in arrestees' urine more frequently than those of any other drug.

Although some studies have shown marijuana to inhibit aggressive behavior and violence, the National Research Council concluded that the "long-term use of marijuana may alter the nervous system in ways that do promote violence." No place serves as a better example than Amsterdam.

Marijuana advocates often point to the Netherlands as a well-functioning society with a relaxed attitude toward drugs, but they rarely mention that Amsterdam is one of Europe's most violent cities. In Amsterdam, officials are in the process of closing marijuana dispensaries, or "coffee shops," because of the crime associated with their operation. Furthermore, the Dutch Ministry of Health, Welfare and Sport has expressed "concern about drug and alcohol use among young people and the social consequences, which range from poor school performance and truancy to serious impairment, including brain damage."

Amsterdam's experience is already being duplicated in California under the current medical marijuana statute. In Los Angeles, police report that areas surrounding cannabis clubs have experienced a 200 percent increase in robberies, a 52.2 percent increase in burglaries, a 57.1 percent increase in aggravated assault, and a 130.8 percent increase in burglaries from automobiles. Current law requires a doctor's prescription to procure marijuana; full legalization would likely spark an even more acute increase in crime.

Legalization of marijuana would also inflict a series of negative consequences on neighborhoods and communities. The nuisance caused by the powerful odor of mature marijuana plants is already striking California municipalities. The city council of Chico, California, has released a report detailing the situation and describing how citizens living near marijuana cultivators are disturbed by the incredible stink emanating from the plants.

Perhaps worse than the smell, crime near growers is increasing, associated with "the theft of marijuana from yards where it is being grown." As a result, housing prices near growers are sinking.

The Practical Matter of Regulation

Theoretical arguments in favor of marijuana legalization usually overlook the practical matter of how the drug would be regulated and sold. It is the details of implementation, of course, that will determine the effect of legalization on families, schools, and communities. Most basically, how and where would marijuana be sold?

- Would neighborhoods become neon red-light districts like Amsterdam's, accompanied by the same crime and social disorder?

- If so, who decides what neighborhoods will be so afflicted—residents and landowners or far-off government officials?

- Or would marijuana sales be so widespread that users could add it to their grocery lists?

- If so, how would stores sell it, how would they store it, and how would they prevent it from being diverted into the gray market?

- Would stores dealing in marijuana have to fortify their facilities to reduce the risk of theft and assault?

The most likely result is that the drug will not be sold in legitimate stores at all, because while the federal government is currently tolerating medical marijuana dispensaries, it will not tolerate wide-scale sales under general legalizational statutes. So marijuana will continue to be sold on the gray or black market.

The act does not answer these or other practical questions regarding implementation. Rather, it leaves those issues to localities. No doubt, those entities will pass a variety of laws in an attempt to deal with the many problems caused by legalization, unless the local laws are struck down by California courts as inconsistent with the underlying initiative, which would be even worse. At best, that patchwork of laws, differing from one locality to another, will be yet another unintended and predictable problem arising from legalization as envisioned under this act.

The Harms of Legalization

Citizens also should not overlook what may be the greatest harms of marijuana legalization: increased addiction to and use of harder drugs. In addition to marijuana's harmful effects on the body and relationship to criminal conduct, it is a gateway drug that can lead users to more dangerous drugs. Prosecutors, judges, police officers, detectives, parole or probation officers, and even defense attorneys know that the vast majority of defendants arrested for violent crimes test positive for illegal drugs, including marijuana. They also know that marijuana is the starter drug of choice for most criminals. Whereas millions of Americans consume moderate amounts of alcohol without ever "moving on" to dangerous drugs, marijuana use and cocaine use are strongly correlated.

While correlation does not necessarily reflect causation, and while the science is admittedly mixed as to whether it is the drug itself or the people the new user associates with who cause the move on to cocaine, heroin, LSD [lysergic acid diethylamide], or other drugs, the RAND Corporation reports that marijuana prices and cocaine use are directly linked, suggesting a substitution effect between the two drugs. Moreover, according to RAND, legalization will cause marijuana prices to fall as much as 80 percent. That can lead to significant consequences because "a 10-percent decrease in the price of marijuana would increase the prevalence of cocaine use by 4.4 to 4.9 percent." As cheap marijuana floods the market both in and outside of California, use of many different types of drugs will increase, as will marijuana use.

It is impossible to predict the precise consequences of legalization, but the experiences of places that have eased restrictions on marijuana are not positive. Already, California is suffering crime, dislocation, and increased drug use under its current regulatory scheme. Further liberalizing the law will only make matters worse.

"The critical determinant of violence is whether an industry is legal, as the history of alcohol prohibition illustrates."

Marijuana Legalization Leads to a Reduction in Crime

Jeffrey A. Miron

In the following viewpoint, Jeffrey A. Miron argues that not only does the legalization of marijuana not lead to an increase in crime, but also there is reason to believe it decreases crime. Miron claims that the marijuana policy in the Netherlands is proof that legalization does not increase crime, citing his peaceful experience in Amsterdam's red-light district as indication that legalization (or something like it, in the case of the Netherlands) is a good thing. Miron is senior lecturer and director of undergraduate studies in the Department of Economics at Harvard University as well as a senior fellow at the Cato Institute.

As you read, consider the following questions:

1. According to the author, what former White House staff member believes the Dutch policy on marijuana is flawed?

Jeffrey A. Miron, "Marijuana, Sex and Amsterdam," *Huffington Post* (blog), September 5, 2013. Copyright © 2013 Jeffrey A. Miron. All rights reserved. Reproduced with permission.

2. What is the main reason for the association between violence and drugs, prostitution, gambling, or any banned good, according to Miron?

3. Which country, according to Miron, in 2009 had a lower past-year marijuana-use rate—the Netherlands or the United States?

For the past twenty years, I have researched the economics of drug legalization versus drug prohibition. Based on this work and much other evidence, I have come to regard legalization as a policy no-brainer. Virtually all the effects would be positive, with minimal risks of significant negatives.

Marijuana Policy in the Netherlands

An important piece of that research has been examination of drug policy in the Netherlands, where marijuana is virtually, although not quite technically, legal. Until recently, however, I had never visited that country.

That changed last month [in August 2013] when my wife, college-age offspring, and I spent a week in Amsterdam. The trip was not an excuse to smoke marijuana in the city's famous coffee shops; despite my pro-legalization position, I do not consume illegal drugs (dry martinis are another story).

Instead, we chose Amsterdam because it is an interesting city we hadn't visited (and because we had frequent flier miles for non-stop flights). We visited the standard tourist destinations such as the Van Gogh Museum and the Anne Frank House, enjoyed rijsttafel (Dutch-Indonesian smorgasbord) and Dutch beer, and avoided being run over (just barely) by the 600,000 bicycles in Amsterdam.

I also visited the famed red-light district, which hosts numerous marijuana-selling coffee shops and legal prostitution (with my wife by side; draw your own conclusions). Legalization advocates point to Amsterdam as evidence that legalization works, at least for marijuana. Legalization critics, such as former White House drug czar Gil Kerlikowske, believe instead that Dutch policy is flawed, generating crime and nuisance effects. Only firsthand observation could give me a clear view of which description is more accurate.

Beauty is often in the eye of the beholder, so die-hard prohibitionists might be unconvinced by my observations until they visit Amsterdam for themselves.

An Absence of Violence

To my eye, however, the red-light district could not have felt safer or more normal. Yes, marijuana was widely available. And yes, sexual services of all manner were openly for sale.

But nothing about the district felt unsafe, or suggested elevated crime or violence; I have felt less safe in many American and European cities. The area is full of young people, including many tourists, having fun or in search of it. Some were undoubtedly under the influence of marijuana or alcohol, or taking other risks. None of this "risk-taking," however, was harming anyone else.

The absence of violence is not surprising. Prohibition, not drug use, is the main reason for the association between violence and drugs, prostitution, gambling, or any banned good. In a legal market, participants resolve disputes with lawyers, courts, and arbitration. In an illegal market, they cannot use these methods and resort to violence instead.

Thus the critical determinant of violence is whether an industry is legal, as the history of alcohol prohibition illustrates. That industry was violent during the 1920–1933 period, when the federal and many state governments banned alcohol, but not before or after. And if the government banned tobacco, or coffee, or ice cream, or any good with substantial demand and imperfect substitutes, a violent black market would arise.

Legalization and Use

Prohibition advocates might still oppose Dutch marijuana policy because they regard all use as undesirable, even if it

Crime in Denver County, Colorado, After Marijuana Legalization, January 1, 2014

	Type of Offense	Jan 1–Dec 31, 2013	Jan 1–Dec 31, 2014	Change
Violent crime	Homicide	41	31	-10 (-24.4%)
	Rape	444	433	-11 (-2.5%)
	Robbery	1,133	1,096	-37 (-3.3%)
	Aggravated Assault	2,368	2,385	17 (0.7%)
	Subtotal	**3,986**	**3,945**	**-41 (-1.0%)**
Property	Burglary	4,975	4,500	-475 (-9.5%)
	Larceny (Except Theft from Motor Vehicle)	7,905	8,003	98 (1.2%)
	Theft from Motor Vehicle	6,572	5,139	-1,433 (-21.8%)
	Auto Theft	3,410	3,373	-37 (-1.1%)
	Arson	94	124	30 (31.9%)
	Subtotal	**22,956**	**21,139**	**-1,817 (-7.9%)**
	Total	**26,942**	**25,084**	**-1,858 (-6.9%)**

TAKEN FROM: Denver Police, Uniform Crime Reporting, January 23, 2015.

generates no harm to third parties. Standard economics predicts that, other things equal, prohibitions reduce use by raising drug prices. But nothing in economics says price is the only determinant of use; for many consumers, other factors matter more.

And again, evidence from the Netherlands is informative. In 2009, the past-year marijuana-use rate was 11.3 percent in the United States but only 7.0 percent in the Netherlands. This does not prove that legalization lowers drug use; many other factors are at play. But these data hardly support the claim that prohibition has a material impact in reducing use.

When we toured Amsterdam on a canal barge, the guide commented that, "Despite legal drugs and prostitution, Amsterdam is a safe city." My son, who has heard me rant about prohibition for years, looked up and quipped, "He should have said, 'Because drugs and prostitution are legal,' right?"

Exactly.

Periodical and Internet Sources Bibliography

The following articles have been selected to supplement the diverse views presented in this chapter.

Paul Armentano	"Debunking the Latest Pathetic Fear Smear Campaign Against Marijuana," AlterNet, February 22, 2015.
Christian Science Monitor	"The Real Marijuana Story," June 5, 2014.
Matt Ferner	"Marijuana May Be the Least Dangerous Recreational Drug, Study Shows," *Huffington Post*, February 24, 2015.
Christopher Ingraham	"Marijuana May Be Even Safer than Previously Thought, Researchers Say," *Washington Post*, February 23, 2015.
Roxanne Khamsi	"How Safe Is Recreational Marijuana?," *Scientific American*, May 14, 2013.
Olga Khazan	"Is Marijuana More Addictive than Alcohol?," *Atlantic*, September 17, 2014.
Gavin McInnes	"Legalize Pot. It's Bad for You," *Intercollegiate Review*, March 10, 2014.
David W. Murray	"Why We Believe Marijuana Is Dangerous," Hudson Institute, November 7, 2014.
Jeff Nesbit	"Is Marijuana Harmful?," *U.S. News & World Report*, October 7, 2014.
Owen Poindexter	"12 of the Biggest Myths About Marijuana Debunked," AlterNet, May 9, 2014.
Joanna Rothkopf	"Study: Marijuana Is Even Less Dangerous than We Thought," *Salon*, February 23, 2015.

CHAPTER 3

Should Use of Medical Marijuana Be Legal?

Chapter Preface

As of 2015, twenty-three states and the District of Columbia had enacted laws that allowed the use of medical marijuana, and several other states continued to debate the issue. California was the first state to implement a law legalizing marijuana for medical use. Looking at the history of medical marijuana in California illustrates some of the issues and debates about legalizing the use of marijuana as medicine.

California Proposition 215, or the Compassionate Use Act of 1996, was passed by California voters on November 5, 1996. The law removed state-level criminal penalties on the use, possession, and cultivation of marijuana by patients, where such use "has been recommended by a physician who has determined that the person's health would benefit from the use of marijuana." Debate about the law was intense and just over 55 percent of voters approved it. Implementing the law raised a whole new host of issues for public debate.

In response to concern about the lack of guidelines for medical marijuana use within the proposition, in 2003 the California legislature passed Senate Bill 420, which put into place guidelines for legal medical marijuana use in California. Among its regulations, the bill created a voluntary identification card program for qualified medical marijuana users, to "provide needed guidance to law enforcement officers" so that legal users could "avoid unnecessary arrest and prosecution." The bill also placed a limit on marijuana possession for each patient to "eight ounces of dried marijuana" and "no more than six mature or 12 immature marijuana plants." In addition, the bill allowed for patients to "cultivate marijuana for medical purposes" through nonprofit collectives or cooperatives, making such transactions subject to sales tax.

One of the main challenges of implementing legal medical marijuana in California was and still is the existence of medical marijuana dispensaries. Although dispensaries are supposed to operate as cooperatives or collectives, the easy membership and cash sales often blur the line with a traditional business. Marijuana dispensaries have been unpopular with many neighbors and law enforcement officers, so much so that in 2010 Los Angeles County banned them. Several other cities and counties followed suit. In 2013 the Supreme Court of California ruled that local governments are allowed to prevent marijuana dispensaries from operating if they decide it is in the best interest of the community.

Another key challenge faced by California and other states that have legalized the medical use of marijuana is the fact that such state legislation conflicts with federal legislation restricting the use of marijuana. The 1970 Controlled Substances Act (CSA) established a federal regulatory system designed to combat recreational drug abuse by making it unlawful to manufacture, distribute, dispense, or possess marijuana and other drugs. Although the US Department of Justice issued a memorandum in 2013 directing US attorneys general to limit investigative and prosecutorial resources to significant threats in states where it is legal, the tension between state laws and federal law continues to cause confusion. As recently as December 2014, the Drug Enforcement Administration (DEA) raided two legal marijuana dispensaries in Los Angeles.

As the experience of California illustrates, even once the issue of state law has been decided, there are a host of other controversial issues involving the regulation of medical marijuana. The authors of the viewpoints in the following chapter debate the various controversies about legalizing medical marijuana and establishing regulations for legal use.

> *"Marijuana has been used throughout the world for thousands of years, and its medicinal benefits are incontrovertible."*

Marijuana Should Be Legalized for Medical Use

Drug Policy Alliance

In the following viewpoint, the Drug Policy Alliance argues that marijuana is safe and effective as a medicine for the treatment of many illnesses. The alliance reports that because of this and the change in public opinion, about half the states now allow the use of medical marijuana. The author claims that the federal government should not interfere with the states and should do more to support research about medical marijuana. The Drug Policy Alliance is a national advocacy leader of drug law reform that is grounded in science, compassion, health, and human rights.

As you read, consider the following questions:

1. According to the Drug Policy Alliance, what two states most recently adopted laws to legalize the use of medical marijuana?

Drug Policy Alliance, "Medical Marijuana," Drugpolicy.org, January 2015, pp. 1–3. Copyright © 2015 Drug Policy Alliance. All rights reserved. Reproduced with permission.

2. What are at least two of the medical conditions that the author claims can be effectively treated by use of medical marijuana?

3. In what way has the Drug Enforcement Administration (DEA) and National Institute on Drug Abuse (NIDA) created a catch-22, according to the author?

Since the 1990s, polls have shown public support for medical marijuana ranging from 70 to 80 percent. Twenty-three states, one U.S. territory (Guam), and the District of Columbia have legalized medical marijuana. Thirteen jurisdictions did so by popular vote—Alaska (58% voter approval), Arizona (65%), California (56%), Colorado (54%), Guam (56%), Maine (61%), Massachusetts (63%), Michigan (63%), Montana (62%), Nevada (65%), Oregon (55%), Washington State (59%) and Washington, D.C. (69%)—while Connecticut, Delaware, Hawaii, Illinois, Maryland, Minnesota, New Hampshire, New Jersey, New Mexico, New York, Rhode Island and Vermont did so through the legislative process.

State Medical Marijuana Laws

State medical marijuana programs vary in significant ways, but most are tightly controlled and regulated by the state health departments. All but one (Washington State) issue identification cards to patients, which help law enforcement recognize who is a valid medical marijuana patient. Seventeen states and D.C. regulate and license centers that produce and dispense marijuana to patients (or will begin doing so in the near future). In California, medical marijuana production and distribution is regulated locally.

The two most recent states to legalize medical marijuana, New York and Minnesota, adopted more limited laws. For example, Minnesota does not allow access to or use of the raw marijuana plant, and neither state permits smoking marijuana—in spite of the strong scientific evidence about the efficacy of smoked marijuana in whole plant form. While these two states' new laws will help thousands of patients, they could be significantly strengthened to provide relief for thousands more.

States that have adopted medical marijuana laws have experienced few, if any, significant problems. Several recent studies have found that medical marijuana laws do not result in an increase—and might actually result in a *decrease*—in rates of marijuana use as well as traffic fatalities, prescription overdose deaths, suicides, and crime rates.

The Safety and Efficacy of Medical Marijuana

Marijuana has been used throughout the world for thousands of years, and its medicinal benefits are incontrovertible, now proven by decades of peer-reviewed, controlled studies published in highly respected medical journals. Marijuana has been shown to alleviate symptoms of a wide range of debilitating medical conditions, including cancer, HIV/AIDS, multiple sclerosis, Alzheimer's disease, post-traumatic stress disorder (PTSD), epilepsy, Crohn's disease, and glaucoma, and is often an effective alternative to narcotic painkillers.

Evidence of marijuana's efficacy in treating severe and intractable pain is particularly impressive. Researchers at the University of California conducted a decade of randomized, double-blind, placebo-controlled clinical trials on the medical utility of inhaled marijuana, concluding that marijuana should be a "first line treatment" for patients with painful neuropathy, who often do not respond to other available treatments. In 1999, the White House commissioned the national Institute of Medicine (IOM) to conduct a two-year review of the scientific data then available with respect to marijuana's potential medical benefits. The study team concluded that, "nausea, appetite loss, pain and anxiety . . . all can be mitigated by marijuana."

More recent research has only confirmed marijuana's broad spectrum of medicinal benefits, even finding that marijuana has potent anti-cancer properties and could one day help unlock new cancer treatments.

The Federal Government

Under our federalist system of government, there are independent state and federal laws regarding marijuana. A state may choose to pass laws making the use of medical marijuana legal under its own laws. Nevertheless, the use of marijuana for any reason remains illegal under federal law, and the federal government retains its ability to arrest and prosecute patients under federal law even if their actions are legal under state law.

Until recently, this situation presented major difficulties for states trying to regulate medical marijuana, leaving lawful patients, and especially providers, vulnerable to arrest and interference from federal law enforcement. However, in August of 2013, the Department of Justice (DOJ) announced that it will allow states to implement laws that legally regulate the production, distribution and sale of marijuana at the state level. The DOJ issued a directive to U.S. attorneys across the country outlining federal objectives for enforcing marijuana laws in states where it is now legal. While reserving the right to challenge state laws in the future, and to enforce federal laws under certain circumstances, the federal government will coordinate with states rather than interfere unless states fail to meet certain core federal priorities, such as preventing access to marijuana by minors, diversion of marijuana to neighboring states, revenue going to criminal enterprises, increases in violence or drugged driving, and damage to public lands.

The Drug Enforcement Administration (DEA) and National Institute on Drug Abuse (NIDA) have created a catch-22 for patients, doctors and scientists by denying that marijuana is a medicine because it is not approved by the Food and

Where Medical Marijuana Is Legal in the United States

■ Medical marijuana is legal

TAKEN FROM: Drug Policy Alliance, "Medical Marijuana,"
January 2015.

Drug Administration (FDA)—while simultaneously obstructing the very research required for marijuana to gain FDA approval.

Marijuana remains the *only* Schedule I drug that DEA prohibits from being produced by private laboratories for scientific research. While there is a plethora of scientific research establishing marijuana's safety and efficacy, NIDA and DEA have effectively blocked the standard FDA development process that would allow for the marijuana plant to be brought to market as a prescription medicine. Although DEA licenses multiple privately funded manufacturers of all other Schedule I drugs, it permits just one facility—operated by NIDA—to supply marijuana to scientists. NIDA has refused to provide marijuana for several major FDA-approved studies.

The Drug Policy Alliance [DPA] played a primary role in the passage of medical marijuana laws in eleven states, starting with California's Proposition 215 in 1996. DPA is committed to increasing the number of states that allow for medical use under state law, strengthening existing state medical marijuana programs, protecting patients from criminal sanctions and discrimination, ending the federal prohibition of marijuana, and ultimately removing marijuana from the federal Controlled Substances Act of 1970 to facilitate research, ensure patient access and allow for marijuana's legal regulation.

"*Legalizing the marijuana plant . . . and allowing open access to it is not necessary and may even create a public health danger for seriously ill patients.*"

The Marijuana Plant Should Not Be Legalized for Medical Use

Drug Free America Foundation, Inc. (DFAF)

In the following viewpoint, the Drug Free America Foundation, Inc. (DFAF) argues that there is no justification for legalizing use of the marijuana plant as medicine. DFAF claims that there is already a synthetic marijuana-component pharmaceutical product on the market prescribed for medical purposes, and more research is under way for potential effective and safe use of natural or synthetic components of the marijuana plant. DFAF is a drug policy and prevention organization committed to creating an environment where citizens live free of illicit drugs.

As you read, consider the following questions:

1. What is the generic name of the pharmaceutical product available in the United States made from synthetic THC, according to DFAF?

Drug Free America Foundation, Inc. (DFAF), "A Briefing Paper on the Evolution of Marijuana to Medicine and a Closer Look at Charlotte's Web," Dfaf.org, January 21, 2014, pp. 1–3, 5. Copyright © 2014 Drug Free America Foundation. All rights reserved. Reproduced with permission.

2. According to the author, Sativex is now approved in how many countries?

3. The author claims that a medicine made from natural THC rather than synthetic THC is in what phase of clinical development in the United States?

Legalizing the crude marijuana plant is not necessary and not a scientific approach to providing safe and effective medicine. A number of modern medicines are derived from plant material, including the marijuana plant. Examples include Taxol, which comes from the yew tree; opiates, which come from the poppy plant; anesthesia, which comes from the coca plant; aspirin, which comes from the willow tree; and dronabinol, which is derived from the marijuana plant.

The Medicinal Component of Marijuana

None of these medicines, however, are the raw plant rolled up and smoked. They are rather derived from specific extracts of the plant and delivered through a safe delivery system in a form that is stable where dosing is known and controllable. Some of these plants, such as the yew, actually contain some compounds that can be deadly, so separating the specific compound that has medicinal value and has been shown to be more beneficial than harmful is extremely important.

Marijuana contains hundreds of compounds, many of which are very harmful to one's health. Marijuana does, however, contain at least one compound, and possibly more, that are supported by science as being medicinal.

Decades ago, the tetrahydrocannabinol (THC) in marijuana was isolated after research proved it to be medically effective. After being isolated from the other compounds, it was synthetically replicated and produced in capsule form. Known as dronabinol generically, it is marketed in the United States under the brand name of Marinol. It is approved by the Food and Drug Administration (FDA) and typically prescribed for appetite stimulation and nausea control associated with chemo and radiation treatment.

Research on Medical Marijuana Efficacy

Another compound in marijuana, cannabidiol (CBD), is currently undergoing research to determine its medical efficacy.

Research is now under way by a European pharmaceutical company GW Pharmaceuticals (GW) to develop a THC-CBD product known as Sativex that is a natural extraction from two marijuana plant strains (one high in THC and one high in CBD), as opposed to a synthetic product. A distinction about the marijuana plants that are cultivated for this research is that the plants are cloned, providing identical plants. GW has developed a safe delivery system rather than promoting the smoking of medicine.

Sativex is now approved in 24 countries. It is indicated as a treatment for symptom improvement in patients with moderate to severe spasticity due to multiple sclerosis (MS) who have not responded adequately to other anti-spasticity medications and who demonstrate clinically significant improvement in spasticity-related symptoms during an initial trial of therapy. Sativex is also in Phase III clinical development for the treatment of cancer pain, the lead indication for the U.S. market. . . .

The Use of Charlotte's Web

Charlotte's Web most often refers to oil extracted from marijuana plants that are bred with the representation that the plants are low in THC (the intoxicating compound in marijuana) and high in CBD content (a nonintoxicating compound in marijuana). The ratio in Charlotte's Web varies, however, and "low in THC" is an uncertain term since it has been reported to have levels of 4–6% and sometimes even higher.

The product getting most of the publicity refers to one of the many marijuana strains cultivated and sold by the Stanley brothers, Joel, Jesse, Jon, Jordan and Jared, in Colorado. It is described as a shorter plant that grows slower than other marijuana plants cultivated at their dispensary. Although the ratio has not been disclosed, it is said to be high in cannabidiol (CBD) and low in tetrahydrocannabinol (THC). How high, and how low is unknown. In their process, they report that the marijuana is soaked in grain alcohol to extract the cannabinoids and then the resulting liquid is put through an evaporator to remove the alcohol. The Stanley brothers report that they named the strain after one of their customers, Charlotte Figi, a young girl with Dravet syndrome. Others report that the name Charlotte's Web comes from the web-like leaves that are distinct to this plant breed.

The Stanley brothers promote Charlotte's Web for use by children through their foundation known as Realm of Caring. Their website, while portraying compassionate photos and personal stories of sick children who they claim have been provided a "better quality of life" through the use of their product, acknowledges that: "*The statements have not been evaluated by the Food and Drug Administration (FDA). These products and statements are not intended to diagnose, treat, cure or prevent any disease. Any and all of Realm of Caring representatives, are not doctors in any way or claim to be.*" . . .

In addition to the product marketed by the Stanleys, a growing number of other dispensaries and online stores market products under the name of Charlotte's Web or as "Low-THC," although sometimes the THC levels have been found to be as high as 15%. Marijuana labeled as "Charlotte's Web" or "Low-THC" varies and consumers have no way of knowing exactly what they are getting.

Potential dangers of using "Charlotte's Web" or "Low-THC" marijuana as a "medicine" are many, including

- There is no standardized dose.

- A patient who takes purported dosage of CBD a day could also be taking unknown amounts of THC.

- These marijuana products could have molds and microbes that are not removed by the ethanol process that converts it into a non-smokable form. (Physicians in Colorado have reported that some children have shown up with bacterial infections, presumed to be from the medical cannabis they are using.)

- There is no way to standardize or purify the compounds in marijuana. In fact, no one knows what the exact THC-CBD ratio is, and the labs that purport to "test" these products are not FDA or DEA [Drug Enforcement Administration] registered. The exact ratio is not identified. The growers are not able to assure batch-to-batch consistency because the plant material is variable, and the manufacturing process itself can affect the CBD-THC ratio.

- We have no way of knowing which patients (ages, diagnoses) have benefited, what side effects they might have experienced, and which patients have gotten no benefit. Only a few "selected" cases are known to have been publicized. All the cases should be reported (without names, of course).

- The product could have harmful chemicals in it that were used in the cultivation (pesticides, herbicides) or extraction processes.

There is a better approach. Following its work with Sativex, GW Pharmaceuticals began to look at the other 99 non-psychoactive cannabinoids in marijuana. Research was conducted using CBD that showed promising results in treating epilepsy. Once published, parents began contacting the researcher asking if they could use this for their children. The researcher then contacted GW. Extensive toxicology research had been done, as well as limited human trials.

GW has continued the research and has developed a product that is basically pure CBD, extracted from cloned marijuana plants, known as Epidiolex. This product is undergoing the necessary scientific scrutiny required of legitimate medicines and is a pure product that overcomes the obstacles listed above. The medication is currently going through the process to obtain approval from the Food and Drug Administration and is now available to patients through clinical trials.

No Need to Legalize the Plant

Legalizing the marijuana plant—even the strain known as Charlotte's Web—and allowing open access to it is not necessary and may even create a public health danger for seriously ill patients.

The THC in marijuana, which science demonstrates has medicinal value, is already available in prescription form as a synthetic medication. A non-synthetic medication containing pure THC is also available in 21 countries and is in Phase III clinical development in the United States. A non-synthetic medication containing pure CBD is now in clinical trials in the United States and available to patients desiring to try the drug.

While GW Pharmaceuticals has obviously led the way in the development of Sativex and Epidiolex, other research is ongoing and it is anticipated that we will see other similar medications brought to market. Efforts should focus on supporting the research and development of modern medicines rather than circumventing our nation's established process for protecting the public from harmful human experiments with substances that could prove to be more harmful than helpful.

VIEWPOINT 3

> *"Relying exclusively on centralized production and distribution is untested and will likely fail to address patients' needs."*

Patients Should Be Allowed to Grow Marijuana Plants for Medicine

Americans for Safe Access

In the following viewpoint, Americans for Safe Access argues that when states legalize the use of medical marijuana, they ought to allow patient cultivation of the marijuana plant as well as provide centralized cultivation. Americans for Safe Access claims personal cultivation can be especially valuable for many poor patients who cannot afford dispensary marijuana, as well as for rural patients who may live far from a marijuana dispensary. Americans for Safe Access is a member-based organization working to ensure safe and legal access to cannabis for therapeutic uses and research.

As you read, consider the following questions:

1. According to the author, federal law imposes harsh mandatory minimum prison sentences for the cultivation of more than how many marijuana plants?

Americans for Safe Access, "Patient Cultivation: The Seed of Safe Access," Safeaccessnow .org, 2011, pp. 2–3. Copyright © 2011 Americans for Safe Access. All rights reserved. Reproduced with permission.

2. Under federal statute, according to Americans for Safe Access, a conviction for possession of 250 grams of marijuana has a sentencing range up to how long?

3. Which state's medical marijuana program that relies upon centralized production has failed to keep up with patient demand, according to the viewpoint?

Restricting patients to a centralized cultivation and distribution system limits their choice and freedom, jeopardizes access in rural areas, subjects large-scale cultivators to lengthy federal sentencing guidelines, and makes medical cannabis unaffordable and out of reach for many qualified patients. Because not all patients have the skill, time or space to cultivate their own cannabis, patients need both centralized and localized cultivation. We must strive to provide the most health care options for patients and to empower them to make their own decisions regarding medical treatment.

Although some states are implementing systems of centralized production and distribution, almost all of these states also allow patients to cultivate their own medical cannabis. Relying exclusively on centralized production and distribution is untested and will likely fail to address patients' needs. In addition, federal law frowns on large-scale cultivation (imposing harsh mandatory minimum prison sentences for more than 100 plants), whereas the federal government rarely goes after individual patient cultivators. Do we really want to rely exclusively on an untested, vulnerable system that is unable to meet patients' needs?

Facts About Marijuana Cultivation

Although most patients prefer to purchase their medication from a local distribution center or have it grown for them, for a state law to work effectively, patients need the right to cultivate as a safety net in case centralized cultivation and the dispensary model do not work.

Cannabis is not a complicated pharmaceutical product; it is a plant that, like a tomato plant, will thrive with appropriate care. While the cultivation of cannabis requires time, resources, and skill, cannabis is still relatively easy to grow. In fact, people have been successfully cultivating cannabis for therapeutic use for thousands of years.

Of the 15 states that regulate medical cannabis [in 2011], only one program prohibits patient cultivation: New Jersey.

Personal cultivation policies allow knowledgeable patients to select cannabis strains that meet their needs and guarantee reliable, affordable, and consistent access to cannabis, especially for patients in rural communities or locales without a dispensing center nearby.

Large-scale cultivation operations are vulnerable to federal scrutiny and could result in arrests and prosecutions. Under federal statute, a conviction for possession of 250 grams (about eight ounces) of cannabis or fewer carries with it a sentencing range of up to six months. However, a defendant convicted under the same statute for possession of 30,000 kilograms (about 1,000 ounces) or more, is subject to a range of 15–25 years.

Restricting patients to a centralized supply with high overhead costs increases the price of medical cannabis and makes it unaffordable for many patients. Patient cultivation ensures prices will be kept low by increasing the options available to patients, which in turn leads to fair and competitive pricing in the medical cannabis market.

Myths and Facts

Myth: Unregulated cultivation will breed diversion and abuse of the medical cannabis program.

Fact: There has been little evidence of diversion among legitimate medical cannabis patients because accountability is inherent in the medical cannabis system. Medical cannabis pa-

California's Medical Marijuana Cultivation Limits

Under Prop. 215 [California Proposition 215], patients are entitled to whatever amount of marijuana is necessary for their personal medical use. However, patients are likely to be arrested if they exceed the SB 420 [California Senate Bill 420] guidelines. SB 420 sets a baseline statewide guideline of 6 mature or 12 immature plants, and 1/2 pound (8 oz.) processed cannabis per patient. Individual cities and counties are allowed to enact higher, but not lower, limits than the state standard. . . . Patients can be exempted from the limits if their physician specifically states that they need more for their own personal use.

California NORML, "California NORML Patient's Guide to Medical Marijuana," November 2013.

tients are sick and need their medication, and typically do not wish to risk losing that privilege by diverting their medication to the illicit market.

Myth: Dispensaries alone will satisfy the demands of the patient community.

Fact: Many patients cannot afford the expensive prices set by the dispensary model. Patients need options and the right to affordably grow their own medicine. In addition, by allowing patients to grow their own medication, they can control its production, quality, and consistency. New Mexico's medical cannabis program, which relies heavily on centralized production and distribution, has been operating for more than two years, but has so far failed to meet patient demand. Without the ability to personally cultivate, patients in New Mexico would still be without medication.

Myth: Pharmacological testing is necessary to ensure safe, unadulterated, and consistent medication.

Fact: While pharmacological testing would improve safety and consistency, at this time it is unrealistic for a number of reasons. Because of the federal government's strict control over cannabis research studies and testing, there is no practical way to carry out such a policy. Given that people have benefited from the therapeutic use of cannabis for thousands of years without pharmacological testing, patients should not have to now suffer because of new, unrealistic standards.

Myth: Patient cultivation increases home invasions and related crimes.

Fact: Concerns over crime associated with patient cultivation are real, but they are often exaggerated by opponents of this issue. The vast majority of medical cannabis crime is connected to dispensaries and outdoor cultivation, and public officials have found that the best way to deal with it is on a case-by-case basis. Furthermore, reasonable regulations can be put in place to better protect patients cultivating in their homes.

Myth: Patient cultivation creates safety and fire hazards.

Fact: The evidence of house fires related to patient cultivation is marginal when considering the amount of cultivation that is actually occurring. Furthermore, the risk of fire hazards can be mitigated by requiring that patients meet certain safety and operational measures prior to their approval to cultivate.

Medical cannabis patients need patient cultivation as a safety net not only to create a functional program, but also to catch members of our community when:

1. The dispensary model does not work for low-income patients who cannot afford expensive dispensary pricing or for rural patients who have to drive hours to the closest dispensary.

2. The Drug Enforcement Administration or other federal agencies attempt to interfere with centralized production and distribution centers.

3. There is a crop failure jeopardizing all of the medication at a centralized cultivation center or pharmacological testing deems all of the medication is unusable.

4. The implementation of the program is stalled or otherwise interrupted, leaving patients without medication.

ASA [Americans for Safe Access] recommends registered patients and their designated caregiver(s) be granted the option to cultivate a small amount of cannabis individually or in small groups so long as they comport with reasonable standards and restrictions set by the appropriate state agency.

> "The U.S. Food and Drug Administration (FDA) has not recognized or approved the marijuana plant as medicine."

Research Does Not Support the Use of the Marijuana Plant as Medicine

National Institute on Drug Abuse

In the following viewpoint, the National Institute on Drug Abuse (NIDA) argues that the US Food and Drug Administration (FDA) has not approved the use of the marijuana plant as medicine because research has not justified the use of the entire plant for medicinal purposes. However, NIDA contends that pharmaceuticals created with cannabinoids have been shown to have medically effective uses and more research is being done in that area. NIDA is part of the National Institutes of Health of the US Department of Health and Human Services, providing national leadership for research on drug abuse and addiction.

As you read, consider the following questions:

1. Approximately how many cannabinoids are in the marijuana plant, according to NIDA?

National Institute on Drug Abuse, "Is Marijuana Medicine?," Drugabuse.gov, April 2015, pp. 1–3. Courtesy of the National Institutes of Health (NIH).

2. For what two purposes does NIDA say the FDA-approved cannabinoid medications are allowed to be used?

3. NIDA claims that scientists are currently studying the use of marijuana and its extracts to treat what diseases?

The term *medical marijuana* refers to using the whole unprocessed marijuana plant or its basic extracts to treat a disease or symptom. The U.S. Food and Drug Administration (FDA) has not recognized or approved the marijuana plant as medicine.

FDA Study of Marijuana

However, scientific study of the chemicals in marijuana, called cannabinoids, has led to two FDA-approved medications that contain cannabinoid chemicals in pill form. Continued research may lead to more medications.

Because the marijuana plant contains chemicals that may help treat a range of illnesses or symptoms, many people argue that it should be legal for medical purposes. In fact, a growing number of states have legalized marijuana for medical use. . . .

The FDA requires carefully conducted studies (clinical trials) in hundreds to thousands of human subjects to determine the benefits and risks of a possible medication. So far, researchers have not conducted enough large-scale clinical trials that show that the benefits of the marijuana plant (as opposed to its cannabinoid ingredients) outweigh its risks in patients it is meant to treat. . . .

The Cannabinoids in Marijuana

Cannabinoids are chemicals related to delta-9-tetrahydrocannabinol (THC), marijuana's main mind-altering ingredient. Other than THC, the marijuana plant contains more than 100 other cannabinoids. Scientists as well as illegal manufacturers have produced many cannabinoids in the lab. Some of these cannabinoids are extremely powerful and have led to serious health effects when abused.

The body also produces its own cannabinoid chemicals. They play a role in regulating pleasure, memory, thinking, concentration, body movement, awareness of time, appetite, pain, and the senses (taste, touch, smell, hearing, and sight).

Currently, the two main cannabinoids from the marijuana plant that are of medical interest are THC and CBD [cannabidiol].

THC increases appetite and reduces nausea. The FDA-approved THC-based medications are used for these purposes. THC may also decrease pain, inflammation (swelling and redness), and muscle control problems.

CBD is a cannabinoid that does not affect the mind or behavior. It may be useful in reducing pain and inflammation, controlling epileptic seizures, and possibly even treating mental illness and addictions.

Recent Research

NIH-funded and other researchers are continuing to explore the possible uses of THC, CBD, and other cannabinoids for medical treatment.

For instance, recent animal studies have shown that marijuana extracts may help kill certain cancer cells and reduce the size of others. Evidence from one cell culture study suggests that purified extracts from whole-plant marijuana can slow the growth of cancer cells from one of the most serious types of brain tumors. Research in mice showed that treatment with purified extracts of THC and CBD, when used with radiation, increased the cancer-killing effects of the radiation.

Scientists are also conducting preclinical and clinical trials with marijuana and its extracts to treat numerous diseases and conditions, such as the following:

- autoimmune diseases (diseases that weaken the immune system):

  - HIV/AIDS

  - multiple sclerosis (MS), which causes gradual loss of muscle control

  - Alzheimer's disease, which causes loss of brain function, affecting memory, thinking, and behavior

- inflammation

- pain

- seizures

- substance use disorders

- mental disorders

Medications Containing Cannabinoids

Two FDA-approved drugs, dronabinol and nabilone, contain THC. They treat nausea caused by chemotherapy and increase appetite in patients with extreme weight loss caused by AIDS.

The United Kingdom, Canada, and several European countries have approved nabiximols (Sativex), a mouth spray containing THC and CBD. It treats muscle control problems caused by MS. The United States is conducting clinical trials for its safe use in treating cancer pain.

Although it has not yet undergone clinical trials, scientists have recently created Epidiolex, a CBD-based liquid drug to treat certain forms of childhood epilepsy.

"*The marijuana measure, which forbids the federal government from using any of its resources to impede state medical marijuana laws, was previously rejected half a dozen times.*"

The Federal Government Has Ended the Ban on Medical Marijuana

Evan Halper

In the following viewpoint, Evan Halper reports that the US federal government has decided to stop enforcing federal drug law prohibiting marijuana use among medical patients in states that have legalized medical marijuana. Halper contends that the move by the federal government reflects a shift in public opinion supporting marijuana legalization, especially for medical use, in spite of the fact that politicians are reluctant to embrace full legalization of marijuana. Halper is a national reporter for the Los Angeles Times.

As you read, consider the following questions:

1. According to Halper, the new federal policy on state medical marijuana legalization marks the emergence of what new alliance?

Evan Halper, "Congress Quietly Ends Federal Government's Ban on Medical Marijuana," *Los Angeles Times*, December 16, 2014. Copyright © 2014 Los Angeles Times. All rights reserved. Reproduced with permission.

2. The author contends that Congress used its authority to block a medical marijuana law from taking effect in Washington, DC, for how many years?

3. According to Halper, are Republican voters more or less likely than the broader public to support outright marijuana legalization?

Tucked deep inside the 1,603-page federal spending measure is a provision that effectively ends the federal government's prohibition on medical marijuana and signals a major shift in drug policy.

The 2015 Spending Bill Provision

The bill's passage over the weekend [December 13–14, 2014] marks the first time Congress has approved nationally significant legislation backed by legalization advocates. It brings almost to a close two decades of tension between the states and Washington over medical use of marijuana.

Under the provision, states where medical pot is legal would no longer need to worry about federal drug agents raiding retail operations. Agents would be prohibited from doing so.

The [Barack] Obama administration has largely followed that rule since last year as a matter of policy. But the measure approved as part of the spending bill, which President Obama plans to sign this week, will codify it as a matter of law.

Pot advocates had lobbied Congress to embrace the administration's policy, which they warned was vulnerable to revision under a less tolerant future administration.

More important, from the standpoint of activists, Congress' action marked the emergence of a new alliance in marijuana politics: Republicans are taking a prominent role in backing states' rights to allow use of a drug the federal government still officially classifies as more dangerous than cocaine.

"This is a victory for so many," said the measure's coauthor, Republican Rep. Dana Rohrabacher of Costa Mesa [California]. The measure's approval, he said, represents "the first time in decades that the federal government has curtailed its oppressive prohibition of marijuana."

The Legalization of Marijuana

By now, 23 states and the District of Columbia have legalized pot or its ingredients to treat ailments, a movement that began in the 1990s. Even back then, some states had been approving broader decriminalization measures for two decades.

The medical marijuana movement has picked up considerable momentum in recent years. The Drug Enforcement Administration, however, continues to place marijuana in the most dangerous category of narcotics, with no accepted medical use.

Congress for years had resisted calls to allow states to chart their own path on pot. The marijuana measure, which forbids the federal government from using any of its resources to impede state medical marijuana laws, was previously rejected half a dozen times. When Washington, D.C., voters approved medical marijuana in 1998, Congress used its authority over the city's affairs to block the law from taking effect for 11 years.

Even as Congress has shifted ground on medical marijuana, lawmakers remain uneasy about full legalization. A separate amendment to the spending package, tacked on at the behest of anti-marijuana crusader Rep. Andy Harris (R-Md.), will jeopardize the legalization of recreational pot in Washington, D.C., which voters approved last month.

Marijuana proponents nonetheless said they felt more confident than ever that Congress was drifting toward their point of view.

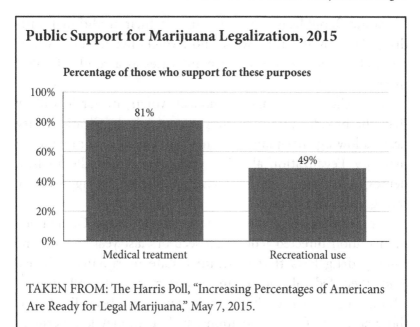

Public Support for Marijuana Legalization, 2015

Percentage of those who support for these purposes

TAKEN FROM: The Harris Poll, "Increasing Percentages of Americans Are Ready for Legal Marijuana," May 7, 2015.

"The war on medical marijuana is over," said Bill Piper, a lobbyist with the Drug Policy Alliance, who called the move historic.

Public Opinion on Legalization

"Now the fight moves on to legalization of all marijuana," he said. "This is the strongest signal we have received from Congress [that] the politics have really shifted. . . . Congress has been slow to catch up with the states and American people, but it is catching up."

The measure, which Rohrabacher championed with Rep. Sam Farr, a Democrat from Carmel [Carmel-by-the-Sea, California], had the support of large numbers of Democrats for years. Enough Republicans joined them this year to put it over the top. When the House first passed the measure earlier this year, 49 Republicans voted aye.

Some Republicans are pivoting off their traditional anti-drug platform at a time when most voters live in states where medical marijuana is legal, in many cases as a result of ballot measures.

Polls show that while Republican voters are far less likely than the broader public to support outright legalization, they favor allowing marijuana for medical use by a commanding majority. Legalization also has great appeal to millennials, a demographic group with which Republicans are aggressively trying to make inroads.

Approval of the pot measure comes after the Obama administration directed federal prosecutors last year to stop enforcing drug laws that contradict state marijuana policies. Since then, federal raids of marijuana merchants and growers who are operating legally in their states have been limited to those accused of other violations, such as money laundering.

"The federal government should never get in between patients and their medicine," said Rep. Barbara Lee (D-Oakland).

"The administration has been behind the curve."

Congress Should Pass a Bill to Reclassify Marijuana for Medical Use

Debra J. Saunders

In the following viewpoint, Debra J. Saunders argues that although Congress has stopped using federal dollars to prosecute medical marijuana dispensaries in states with legal medical marijuana, additional legislation is needed. Saunders contends that Congress should pass the Compassionate Access, Research Expansion, and Respect States Act of 2015 to reclassify marijuana from a Schedule I drug to a Schedule II drug, thereby recognizing its legitimate medical uses. Saunders is a columnist for the San Francisco Chronicle.

As you read, consider the following questions:

1. According to Saunders, what three US senators introduced the Compassionate Access, Research Expansion, and Respect States Act of 2015?

Debra J. Saunders, "Medical Marijuana Bill Lost in Smoke," Spectator.org, March 17, 2015. Copyright © 2015 Creators Syndicate. All rights reserved. Reproduced with permission.

2. What did CNN physician-reporter Sanjay Gupta reveal a couple years ago that changed the debate about medical marijuana?

3. According to Saunders, does President Barack Obama support legal medical marijuana?

Last year [2014], Congress passed an amendment that barred the Department of Justice from using federal dollars to prosecute medical marijuana dispensaries in states that have legalized them. Last week [in March 2015], three senators proposed a measure to clean up the federal-state medical marijuana mess once and for all.

Sens. Cory Booker, D-N.J., Kirsten Gillibrand, D-N.Y., and Rand Paul, R-Ky., introduced their Compassionate Access, Research Expansion, and Respect States Act [also known as the CARERS Act], which should draw support from the right and left. Why? First, it would reclassify marijuana from a Schedule I drug to a Schedule II, granting recognition that marijuana has legitimate medical uses, a sop to the left. Second, it would direct the federal government to stop prosecuting dispensers in states that have legalized marijuana for medical use—a states' rights emphasis that should draw GOP votes. The measure also would allow cannabidiol imports to help patients with epilepsy and seizure disorders—the folks who need medical marijuana the most—and allow [Department of] Veterans Affairs doctors to prescribe medical marijuana. Booker sees his legislation as a matter of "common sense, fiscal prudence and compassion."

For decades, Congress wouldn't move on medical marijuana because D.C. pols thought of advocates as goof-offs who just want to get high. They didn't see the legitimate medical benefits. Then, two years ago, CNN physician-reporter Sanjay Gupta looked at the issue anew and found that cannabis could help children with life-threatening seizures. Medical marijuana has been used to treat people with epilepsy, Parkinson's disease, brain tumors and post-traumatic stress disorder without the serious side effects often associated with prescription drugs.

From San Francisco, the CARERS Act looks like a political slam dunk. It has bipartisan support. Already 23 states have legalized medical marijuana, which puts momentum on the "yes" side. "It stands a good chance of moving because it's so bipartisan in nature," said Bill Piper, the Drug Policy Alliance's man in Washington, D.C. But: "The hard part is going to be getting it through committee." Senate Judiciary Committee chairman Chuck Grassley, R-Iowa, opposes the bill.

Will Grassley allow the bill to come to a vote? "The committee is unlikely to take up a bill in the near future that remakes these laws so broadly," spokeswoman Jill Gerber answered. She added that Grassley "is looking at ways to lift any unnecessary barriers" to scientific research into marijuana-based medicines to treat epilepsy and other conditions affecting children.

There are eleven GOP and nine Democratic senators on the committee. I see three R's who could vote yes; Mike Lee of Utah and Ted Cruz of Texas support states' rights, and Jeff Flake of Arizona voted for similar legislation in the House. Maybe I'm wrong. Maybe there are more.

That would put Sen. Dianne Feinstein in the middle. Other committee Dems are very likely to vote yes. On the one hand, Feinstein and Grassley often work closely on drug war issues. On the other hand, Feinstein does represent California. Her office told me DiFi is still reviewing the legislation.

Which leads to my final question: Would President Barack Obama sign the CARERS Act? Advocates believe that the White House could have and should have made marijuana a Schedule II drug years ago but didn't. The administration has been behind the curve. "Everyone pretty much believes that" Obama is not really for current federal marijuana laws, said

Schedule I and II Drugs

Schedule I

Schedule I drugs, substances, or chemicals are defined as drugs with no currently accepted medical use and a high potential for abuse. Schedule I drugs are the most dangerous drugs of all the drug schedules with potentially severe psychological or physical dependence. Some examples of Schedule I drugs are heroin, lysergic acid diethylamide (LSD), marijuana (cannabis), 3,4-methylenedioxymethamphetamine (ecstasy), methaqualone, and peyote.

Schedule II

Schedule II drugs, substances, or chemicals are defined as drugs with a high potential for abuse, less abuse potential than Schedule I drugs, with use potentially leading to severe psychological or physical dependence. These drugs are also considered dangerous. Some examples of Schedule II drugs are combination products with less than 15 milligrams of hydrocodone per dosage unit (Vicodin), cocaine, methamphetamine, methadone, hydromorphone (Dilaudid), meperidine (Demerol), oxycodone (OxyContin), fentanyl, Dexedrine, Adderall, and Ritalin.

Drug Enforcement Administration (DEA),
"Drug Schedules."

Marijuana Majority chairman Tom Angell, just as many believed Obama supported same-sex marriage back when he said he was against it. "I wouldn't be shocked to see him evolve on this issue the same way he did for marriage equality," Angell mused. "Maybe all we need is for Joe Biden to say that marijuana should be legal."

Periodical and Internet Sources Bibliography

The following articles have been selected to supplement the diverse views presented in this chapter.

Russell Berman	"Why Congress Gave In to Medical Marijuana," *Atlantic*, December 17, 2014.
William Courtney	"Medical Marijuana Is Safe for Children," *U.S. News & World Report*, January 7, 2013.
Shaunacy Ferro	"Sanjay Gupta: 'Sometimes Marijuana Is the Only Thing That Works,'" *Salon*, August 12, 2013.
Conor Friedersdorf	"When States Dare to Decide on Medical Marijuana," *Atlantic*, March 10, 2015.
Josh Harkinson	"The Federal War on Medical Marijuana Is Over," *Mother Jones*, December 16, 2014.
Peter Hecht	"The Politics of Pot and Pain," *National Journal*, April 3, 2014.
Jeffrey Miron	"The Case to Reclassify Grass," *Newsweek*, March 10, 2015.
Alfred Ryan Nerz	"The Federal Government Recognized the Health Benefits of Medical Marijuana 40 Years Ago," *Utne Reader*, July–August 2013.
Jacob Sullum	"Washington's Legal Marijuana Mess," *Reason*, July 2014.
Yvette C. Terrie	"Medical Marijuana: The Myths and Realities," *U.S. News & World Report*, April 14, 2015.
Amelia Thomson-DeVeaux	"Washington's Weed Whackers," *American Prospect*, August 20, 2013.

CHAPTER 4

Should Recreational Use of Marijuana Be Legal?

Chapter Preface

Perhaps unthinkable fifty years ago, the movement to legalize marijuana is gaining momentum in the United States. A Pew Research Center poll in March 2015 found that 53 percent of Americans supported marijuana legalization. This recent tipping point in opinion is reflected in the recent successful voter initiatives around the country to legalize marijuana. In addition, many cities and counties have adopted relaxed policies toward individual marijuana possession for recreational use. Whether or not these recent changes in marijuana policy constitute a nationwide trend remains to be seen.

Voters in Colorado and Washington State passed initiatives in 2012 that legalized the sale and distribution of marijuana for adults twenty-one years of age and older under state law. Oregon and Alaska passed similar initiatives legalizing marijuana in 2014. Also in 2014, the District of Columbia approved Initiative 71, which permits adults twenty-one years of age or older to grow and possess (but not sell) limited amounts of marijuana. Nevada voters will face a similar initiative on their November 2016 ballot and other states are likely to place the issue in front of voters soon. Worldwide, in December 2013, Uruguay became the first country to legalize the production, sale, and use of marijuana.

One issue that arises in the marijuana debate is that of distinguishing between two options for ending marijuana prohibition: legalization and decriminalization. The goal behind marijuana decriminalization is to eliminate criminal penalties for drug possession (although frequently proposals for decriminalization do not apply to drug production), without completely legalizing the drug and having it be regulated by the government akin to alcohol and tobacco. Proponents of decriminalization contend that there are harms from prohibition that could be reduced by a policy of decriminalization.

The famous cannabis cafes in Amsterdam are a result of decriminalization—the Netherlands adopted a policy of decriminalization toward marijuana use in the 1970s but has never officially legalized marijuana use, possession, and sale.

It is too early to gather definitive evidence from the states that have legalized marijuana about its impact. As the authors of the viewpoints in the following chapter illustrate, there is quite a bit of disagreement about the wisdom of legalization and the possible effects to society legalization may pose.

"The social costs of legalizing marijuana would outweigh any possible tax that could be levied."

Research Supports Continued Prohibition of Marijuana

Office of National Drug Control Policy (ONDCP)

In the following viewpoint, the Office of National Drug Control Policy (ONDCP) argues that Congress has determined that marijuana is dangerous and ought to be illegal for good reasons. ONDCP contends that there are currently damaging consequences to society from marijuana use and if it were legal the problems—including the number of prisoners, the economic damages, and the environmental degradation—would only increase. ONDCP advises the president on drug control issues, coordinates drug control activities, and produces the annual National Drug Control Strategy.

As you read, consider the following questions:

1. According to ONDCP, how many Americans meet the diagnostic criteria for abuse of or dependence on marijuana?

Office of National Drug Control Policy (ONDCP), "Answers to Frequently Asked Questions About Marijuana," Whitehouse.gov, December 9, 2010. Courtesy of Whitehouse.gov.

2. What percentage of federal prisoners sentenced for drug offenses were incarcerated for drug trafficking, according to ONDCP?

3. According to the viewpoint, how much greater were alcohol-related costs in 2009 than the federal, state, and local revenues collected on alcohol?

In enacting the Controlled Substances Act (CSA), Congress determined that marijuana is a Schedule I controlled substance. In 2012, voters in Colorado and Washington State also passed initiatives legalizing marijuana for adults 21 and older under state law. As with state medical marijuana laws, it is important to note that Congress has determined that marijuana is a dangerous drug and that the illegal distribution and sale of marijuana is a serious crime. The Department of Justice (DOJ) is committed to enforcing the CSA consistent with these determinations. . . .

The Negative Impact of Marijuana Use

Marijuana is the most commonly used illicit drug in the United States. In 2011 alone, more than 18 million Americans age 12 and older reported using the drug within the past month. Approximately 4.2 million people met the diagnostic criteria for abuse of or dependence on this drug. This is more than pain relievers, cocaine, tranquilizers, hallucinogens, and heroin combined.

There are very real consequences associated with marijuana use. In 2010, marijuana was involved in more than 461,000 emergency department visits nationwide. This is nearly 39 percent of all emergency department visits involving illicit drugs, and highlights the very real dangers that can accompany use of the drug.

And in 2011, approximately 872,000 Americans 12 or older reported receiving treatment for marijuana use, more than any other illicit drug. Despite some viewpoints that marijuana is harmless, these figures present a sobering picture of this drug's very real and serious harms.

Marijuana places a significant strain on our health care system, and poses considerable danger to the health and safety of the users themselves, their families, and our communities. Marijuana presents a major challenge for health care providers, public safety professionals, and leaders in communities and all levels of government seeking to reduce the drug use and its consequences throughout the country. . . .

Public Discussion About Marijuana

There is significant public discussion around marijuana, much of which includes the terms legalization, decriminalization, and medical marijuana. Below are very general definitions for these terms.

Marijuana Legalization–Laws or policies which make the possession and use of marijuana legal under state law.

Marijuana Decriminalization–Laws or policies adopted in a number of state and local jurisdictions which reduce the penalties for possession and use of small amounts of marijuana from criminal sanctions to fines or civil penalties.

Medical Marijuana–State laws which allow an individual to defend himself or herself against criminal charges of marijuana possession if the defendant can prove a medical need for marijuana under state law.

People in Prison for Marijuana Use

Simply stated, there are very few people in state or federal prison for marijuana-related crimes. It is useful to look at all drug offenses for context. Among sentenced prisoners under state jurisdiction in 2008, 18% were sentenced for drug offenses. We know from the most recent survey of inmates in state prison that only six percent (6%) of prisoners were drug possession offenders, and just over four percent (4.4%) were drug offenders with no prior sentences.

In total, one-tenth of one percent (0.1 percent) of state prisoners were marijuana possession offenders with no prior sentences.

For federal prisoners, who represent 13 percent of the total prison population, about half (51 percent) had a drug offense as the most serious offense in 2009. And federal data show that the vast majority (99.8 percent) of federal prisoners sentenced for drug offenses were incarcerated for drug trafficking.

Many advocates of marijuana legalization point to the significant number of marijuana-related arrests, including for the sale, manufacturing, and possession of the drug, as an unnecessary burden on the criminal justice system. While federal, state, and local laws pertaining to marijuana do lead to criminal justice costs, it is important to understand how decriminalization or legalization might further exacerbate these costs. Alcohol, a legal, carefully regulated substance, provides useful context for this discussion. Arrests for alcohol-related crimes, such as violations of liquor laws and driving under the influence, totaled nearly 2.5 million in 2010—far more than arrests for all illegal drug use, and certainly far more than arrests for marijuana-related crimes. It is therefore fair to suggest that decriminalizing or legalizing marijuana might not reduce the drug's burden to our justice and public health systems with respect to arrests, but might increase these costs by making the drug more readily available, leading to increased use, and ultimately to more arrests for violations of laws controlling its manufacture, sale, and use.

Federal Opposition to Medical Marijuana

It is the federal government's position that marijuana be subjected to the same rigorous clinical trials and scientific scrutiny that the Food and Drug Administration (FDA) applies to all other new medications, a comprehensive process designed to ensure the highest standards of safety and efficacy.

It is this rigorous FDA approval process, not popular vote, that should determine what is, and what is not, medicine. The raw marijuana plant, which contains nearly 500 different chemical compounds, has not met the safety and efficacy standards of this process. According to the Institute of Medicine (IOM), smoking marijuana is an unsafe delivery system that produces harmful effects. . . .

A number of states have passed voter referenda or legislative actions allowing marijuana to be made available for a variety of medical conditions upon a licensed prescriber's recommendation, despite such measures' inconsistency with the scientific thoroughness of the FDA approval process. But these state actions are not, and never should be, the primary test for declaring a substance a recognized medication. Physicians routinely prescribe medications with standardized modes of administration that have been shown to be safe and effective at treating the conditions that marijuana proponents claim are relieved by smoking marijuana. Biomedical research and medical judgment should continue to determine the safety and effectiveness of prescribed medications. . . .

Marijuana Legalization and Drug Trafficking

Violent Mexican criminal organizations derive revenue from more than just marijuana sales. They also produce and traffic methamphetamine and heroin, continue to move significant amounts of cocaine, and conduct an array of criminal activities including kidnapping, extortion, and human trafficking. Because of the variety and scope of the cartels' business, and its illicit and purposefully obscured nature, determining the precise percentage of revenues from marijuana is problematic, but we can be confident that even the complete elimination of one of their illicit "product lines" will not result in disbanding of their criminal organizations.

The existing black market for marijuana will not simply disappear if the drug is legalized and taxed. Researchers from the RAND Corporation have noted a significant profit motive for existing black market providers to stay in the market, as "they can still cover their costs of production and make a nice profit."

With this in mind, it is crucial to reduce demand for marijuana in the United States and work with the government and people of Mexico to continue our shared commitment to defeat violent drug cartels.

Marijuana Legalization and Tax Revenue

While taxing marijuana could generate some revenues for state and local governments, research suggests that the economic costs associated with use of the drug could far outweigh any benefit gained from an increase in tax revenue.

In the United States in 2007, illegal drugs cost $193 billion ($209 billion in 2011 dollars) in health care, lost productivity, crime, and other expenditures. Optimistic evaluations of the potential financial savings from legalization and taxation are often flawed, and fail to account for the considerable economic and social costs of drug use and its consequences.

This issue is particularly relevant in the marijuana debate. For example, the California Board of Equalization estimated that $1.4 billion of potential revenue could arise from legalization. This assessment, according to the RAND Corporation, is "based on a series of assumptions that are in some instances subject to tremendous uncertainty and in other cases not valid."

Another recent report from RAND examines this issue in greater detail. The report concludes that legalization and taxation of marijuana would lead to a decrease in the retail price of the drug, likely by more than 80 percent. While this conclusion is subject to a number of uncertainties, including the effect of legalization on production costs and price and the federal government's response to the state's legalization of a substance that would remain illegal under federal law, it is fair to say that the price of marijuana would drop significantly. And because drug use is sensitive to price, especially among young people, higher prices help keep use rates relatively low.

The existing black market for marijuana will not simply disappear if the drug is legalized and taxed. RAND also noted that "there is a tremendous profit motive for the existing black market providers to stay in the market, as they can still cover their costs of production and make a nice profit." Legalizing marijuana would also place a dual burden on the government of regulating a new legal market while continuing to pay for the negative side effects associated with an underground market, whose providers have little economic incentive to disappear.

Legalization means price comes down; the number of users goes up; the underground market adapts; and the revenue gained through a regulated market most likely will not keep pace with the financial and social cost of making this drug more accessible.

Consider the economic realities of other substances. The tax revenue collected from alcohol pales in comparison to the costs associated with it. Federal excise taxes collected on alcohol in 2009 totaled around $9.4 billion; state and local revenues from alcohol taxes totaled approximately $5.9 billion. Taken together ($15.3 billion), this is just over six percent of the nearly $237.8 billion (adjusted for 2009 inflation) in alcohol-related costs from health care, treatment services, lost productivity, and criminal justice.

While many levels of government and communities across the country are facing serious budget challenges, we must find innovative solutions to get us on a path to financial stability—it is clear that the social costs of legalizing marijuana would outweigh any possible tax that could be levied.

Marijuana Cultivation and the Environment

Outdoor marijuana cultivation creates a host of negative environmental effects. These grow sites affect wildlife, vegetation, water, soil, and other natural resources through the use of chemicals, fertilizers, terracing, and poaching. Marijuana cultivation results in the chemical contamination and alteration of watersheds; diversion of natural water courses; elimination of native vegetation; wildfire hazards; poaching of wildlife; and disposal of garbage, non-biodegradable materials, and human waste.

Marijuana growers apply insecticides directly to plants to protect them from insect damage. Chemical repellants and poisons are applied at the base of the marijuana plants and around the perimeter of the grow site to ward off or kill rats, deer, and other animals that could cause crop damage. Toxic chemicals are applied to irrigation hoses to prevent damage by rodents. According to the National Park Service, "degradation to the landscape includes tree and vegetation clearing, use of various chemicals and fertilizers that pollute the land and contribute to food chain contamination, and construction of ditches and crude dams to divert streams and other water sources with irrigation equipment."

Outdoor marijuana grow site workers can also create serious wildfire hazards by clearing land for planting (which results in piles of dried vegetation) and by using campfires for cooking, heat, and sterilizing water. In August 2009, growers destroyed more than 89,000 acres in the Los Padres National Forest in Southern California. The massive La Brea wildfire began in the Los Padres National Forest within the San Rafael Wilderness area in Santa Barbara County, California, and subsequently spread to surrounding county and private lands. According to United States Forest Service (USFS) reporting, the source of the fire was an illegal cooking fire at an extensive, recurring drug trafficking organization–operated outdoor grow site where more than 20,000 marijuana plants were under cultivation. According to the USFS, suppression and resource damage costs of the La Brea wildfire totaled nearly $35 million.

In addition to the environmental damage, the cost to rehabilitate the land damaged by illicit marijuana grows is prohibitive, creating an additional burden to public and tribal land agency budgets. According to internal Park Service estimates, full cleanup and restoration costs range from $14,900 to $17,700 per acre. Total costs include removal and disposal of hazardous waste (pesticides, fuels, fertilizers, batteries) and removal of camp facilities, irrigation hoses, and garbage. Full restoration includes re-contouring plant terraces, large tent pads, and cisterns/wells and revegetating clear-cut landscapes.

The United States has an abundance of public lands set aside by Congress for conservation, recreational use, and enjoyment of the citizens of this country and visitors from around the globe. Unfortunately, criminal organizations are exploiting some of these public and tribal lands as grow sites for marijuana.

During calendar year 2010, nearly 10 million plants were removed from nearly 24,000 illegal outdoor grow sites nationwide. These numbers provide insight into the size and scale of the negative environmental impact that marijuana cultivation can have on our nation's public lands.

> *"Many in support of marijuana legalization disregard concerns about the potential increases in the availability of marijuana and/or increases in marijuana use should such laws be passed."*

There Would Be Many Negative Effects from Marijuana Legalization

American Society of Addiction Medicine (ASAM)

In the following viewpoint, the American Society of Addiction Medicine (ASAM) argues that research supports the view that marijuana legalization would not have the positive effects many of its proponents claim. Furthermore, ASAM contends that legalization would increase use, thereby increasing the negative effects of use such as addiction, drugged driving, and illicit use by teenagers. ASAM is a professional society of physicians and associated professionals dedicated to improving the quality of addiction treatment and supporting research of addiction.

American Society of Addiction Medicine (ASAM), "White Paper on State-Level Proposals to Legalize Marijuana," Asam.org, July 25, 2012, pp. 7–15. Copyright © 2012 American Society of Addiction Medicine (ASAM). All rights reserved. Reproduced with permission.

As you read, consider the following questions:

1. ASAM claims that research regarding California's proposed marijuana legalization determined that legalization would cause marijuana prices to drop by up to what percentage?

2. The author cites government research determining that the annual social cost of tobacco outweighs tax revenue by how much?

3. According to ASAM, in what year did daily marijuana use among twelfth graders reach a thirty-year high?

Marijuana legalization has been promoted as a public health and safety measure, as a way to decrease drug-related crime, and as a solution to the harms caused by marijuana criminalization, including incarceration, among others. In particular, those who advocate for the legalization of marijuana commonly argue that marijuana legalization will significantly reduce the illegal trade of marijuana and the crime associated with that illegal trade. They further anticipate that legal marijuana will be a significant source of tax revenue, and it will reduce the high costs related to law enforcement. These claims have not been validated, in part because the full consequences of marijuana legalization remain unknowable; however, there exists valuable, independent, but limited, prospective research on the likely outcomes of state-based marijuana legalization in the US.

Research About Marijuana Legalization in California

The RAND Corporation analyzed the prospective effects of legalized marijuana under passage of California's Proposition 19 [also known as the Regulate, Control and Tax Cannabis Act] in 2010 with the continued federal prohibition of marijuana. Researchers concluded that rates of marijuana use in that state would substantially increase. Prohibition of drugs, including marijuana, currently increases the cost of doing business because of the many risks it places on producers and sellers. Under state legalization, the price of marijuana would drop significantly—up to 80%—with the market price for users depending on taxes and regulation. A "gray market" would still exist for non-taxed, unregulated marijuana. The black market potential for marijuana is great, as the United States has learned from tobacco that is smuggled illegally over the Canada-US border. The specific design of state legalization would dramatically impact projected taxes collected and rates of use, including how high a tax is used, differences in taxes and regulation of potency, home cultivation of the drug, advertising, and the development and management of the regulatory system put in place. This would be in conflict with federal law under which marijuana still would be illegal.

Another RAND study concluded that marijuana legalization in California would not significantly reduce Mexican drug trafficking organizations' (DTOs') gross revenue, nor would it significantly reduce drug-related violence in Mexico. Researchers noted that "the only way Prop 19 could importantly cut DTO drug *export* revenues is if California-produced marijuana is smuggled to other states at prices that outcompete current Mexican supplies." Diverted marijuana from legal production in one state has implications for all others, as it would undercut marijuana prices across the country.

The price elasticity of marijuana under a legalization scheme is complicated because addictive substances do not behave in the market the same way nonaddictive substances do. Demand for marijuana changes from a perceived luxury with first-time use to a virtual necessity for those users who have marijuana dependence. For the nondependent marijuana user, demand is sensitive to changes in price. Marketing to customers has potential under both legalization and decriminalization scenarios to drive up the market. Should the legalization of commercial sales of marijuana be accompanied by legalization of advertising of commercially sold marijuana, the evidence that tobacco cigarette advertising increases consumption suggests that the same effect on demand may be true for marijuana. Levels of exposure to cigarette advertising impact adolescent smoking behaviors, with high exposure to cigarette advertising increasing the likelihood of smoking. There is also evidence that alcohol advertising increases alcohol consumption, and separately, that bans against advertising alcohol have varying effects on reducing use.

ASAM [American Society of Addiction Medicine] recognizes that while the studies of prospective marijuana legalization described here relate specifically to California, the findings are likely applicable to other states, should legalization initiatives pass and be implemented. If marijuana were legalized in any state, there would likely be changes—both expected and unexpected—in price, taxes, and marketing within that state and in surrounding states.

Criminal Penalties for Marijuana

In addition to collecting revenues, state-based marijuana legalization initiatives seek to mitigate the harmful effects of current criminal justice sanctions related to marijuana, as there is a widely held perception that the public health harms of criminal justice interventions are greater than their benefits. The United States has one of the highest rates of incarceration in the world, with 7.2 million people under supervision of the criminal justice system, of which 5.5 million people are on probation and parole. In a sample of male arrestees from ten sites in the US, more than half tested positive for illicit drugs at the time of arrest, ranging from 64–81%, demonstrating the ongoing connection between crime and drug use. Drug use often continues after release and is tied to high rates of recidivism while under community supervision. Marijuana was the most common drug identified among offenders with

36–56% testing positive. In terms of the role of marijuana sale in incarceration, the majority of individuals in state and federal prison for marijuana offenses are neither "unambiguously low-level" nor are they "kingpins" in the drug trade. Further study confirmed that an estimated 0.5% of all incarcerated individuals served time for their marijuana use; the vast majority of individuals incarcerated for marijuana possession were involved in distribution. Similarly, analysis by the National Center on Addiction and Substance Abuse at Columbia University (CASAColumbia) showed that only 2% of all incarcerated persons in the nation's prisons and jails were incarcerated due to a marijuana charge as the controlling offense. Controlling offenses of marijuana possession accounted for 1.1% of all incarcerated persons while 0.9% of all inmates were incarcerated for marijuana possession as their only offense.

Arrests for marijuana possession account for 45.8% of all drug-related arrests, totaling 750,000 arrests in 2010. Based on the number of people serving time for marijuana offenses compared to the number of sellers, researchers have concluded that, despite the many arrests for possession, "marijuana toughness" is low in the US. The likelihood that at present, marijuana sellers will spend time incarcerated is very low compared to sellers of other illicit drugs such as cocaine and heroin; therefore, "easing up on toughness" of marijuana laws would not substantially reduce incarceration rates and its substantial costs, though it is unclear what would be the full impact of marijuana legalization on this population. Removing criminal penalties for marijuana possession (i.e., marijuana decriminalization) could substantially reduce the large number of marijuana possession arrests depending upon laws regarding limitations on possession, use, transportation, etc. Likewise, under marijuana legalization, marijuana possession arrests would likely plummet in those states; however, under both circumstances, other marijuana-related arrests would still be made.

Negative Consequences of Marijuana Legalization

Any state considering changing the legal status of marijuana should consider the negative health consequences of such changes, as well as the benefits of maintaining the criminalization of marijuana sale and use.

Advocates for marijuana legalization often promote as a reason to legalize marijuana the fact that the costs of alcohol and tobacco far outweigh those of marijuana. ASAM recognizes that at present, legal drugs like alcohol and tobacco are more widely used and cause substantial—and significantly more, in many cases—harm than marijuana and in some cases, more harm than all of the illegal drugs combined. The nonmedical use of prescription drugs is now the fastest growing drug problem in the United States. These legal drugs provide evidence that drug use itself—not its illegality—is a national public health threat. Legal drugs currently wreak havoc on public health, producing substantial financial and health burdens. The White House Office of National Drug Control Policy (ONDCP) affirmed that, "The health care and criminal justice costs associated with alcohol and tobacco far surpass the tax revenue they generate, and little of the taxes collected on these substances is contributed to the offset of their substantial social and health costs." The annual social cost in the US of alcohol is estimated at between $185 and $235 billion and for tobacco at $200 billion. Those costs vastly exceed the value of US tax revenue from the sale of these two substances ($14 billion for alcohol and $25 billion for tobacco). The same would likely be true for legal marijuana. The College on Problems of Drug Dependence (CPDD) acknowledges, "At present levels of use, the health costs [illegal drugs] impose on users and on society are dwarfed . . . by those attributable to tobacco (nicotine) and alcohol. The health costs of illicit drugs might well approach or exceed those of tobacco and alcohol if their legal status were changed and their use increased sharply."

Revenues from taxes on alcohol and tobacco currently do not approach the costs of prevention and treatment. It is also unclear how significant would be the cost of setting up a regulatory scheme for legal marijuana. Although a possible goal of state-based marijuana legalization could be to increase funding for addiction prevention and treatment through taxation of commercial activities associated with legalized marijuana, such an outcome is far from likely to be achieved as can be seen from the use of tax revenue from legal alcohol and tobacco; moreover, the negative health effects of increased marijuana use would substantially escalate.

The Challenges of Regulation

There is great uncertainty of anticipated federal government involvement in enforcing federal marijuana laws should marijuana be legalized at the state level. Nationally, there are an estimated 2.7 million alcohol-related arrests each year compared to 750,000 annual marijuana possession arrests. If marijuana use increased, as can be expected under legalization, it is likely that there would be an increase in the number of arrests at the state level for marijuana-related incidents such as public use violations, violations in laws regulating age limits, and marijuana-related arrests for driving under the influence (DUI).

Currently, marijuana is the most common drug involved in drugged driving—a significant cause of highway crashes, injury, and death. New research from meta-analyses shows that marijuana use doubles the risk of a crash; habitual marijuana use is associated with increased risk of crash injury. Among all fatally injured drivers in the US in 2009 for which drug test results were available, 8.6% were positive for marijuana. A study of fatally injured drivers in Washington State showed that 12% were positive for marijuana. A study of seriously injured drivers in Maryland showed that 26.9% were positive for marijuana; 50% of drivers under age 21 were

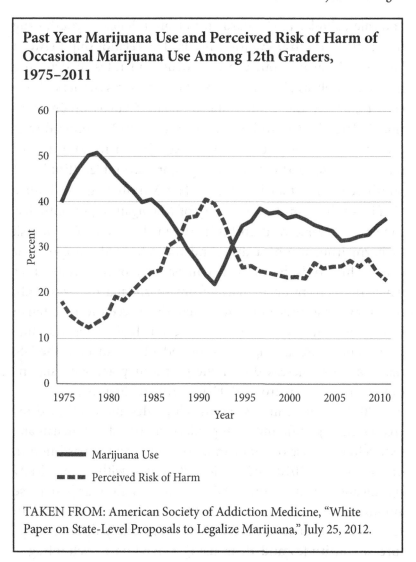

Past Year Marijuana Use and Perceived Risk of Harm of Occasional Marijuana Use Among 12th Graders, 1975–2011

Marijuana Use

Perceived Risk of Harm

TAKEN FROM: American Society of Addiction Medicine, "White Paper on State-Level Proposals to Legalize Marijuana," July 25, 2012.

positive for marijuana. Increases in rates of drugged driving due to marijuana would raise the costs resulting from crashes, injuries, and lost lives. Thus, decreases in highway safety constitute an easy-to-predict negative consequence of the legalization of marijuana use by adults.

Advocates of marijuana legalization commonly support the use of an age limit of 21 for marijuana use, production, and sales, similar to standards for alcohol. Rates of youth drug use instruct youth prevention needs. The relationship between "perceived harm" from use of a drug and rates of drug use has been well established by public health researchers. A recent report by the United States Senate Caucus on International Narcotics Control, released in June 2012, expressed serious concern over recent increases in national rates of marijuana use, particularly noting more favorable attitudes of youth regarding marijuana use. The Monitoring the Future (MTF) study from the University of Michigan importantly has shown an inverse relationship between the perception of risk of harm from use of a drug and the rate of the use of that drug. This study has shown consistently over decades that when the perception of harm from marijuana use was high, marijuana use was low and when the perception of harm from marijuana use was low, the use was high. After a decline in marijuana use among 8th, 10th and 12th graders in the US, marijuana use increased over the past four years, with significant increases seen from 2009 to 2010 for lifetime, past year, past 30 days, and daily use across all grades and continued increases among 10th and 12th graders in 2011. Daily marijuana use, defined as use on 20 or more occasions in the past month, increased from 2010 to 2011 for all grades, with a statistically significant increase from 2007. In 2011, daily marijuana use among 12th graders reached a 30-year high of 6.6% or 1 in 15. (It is important to note that the MTF study does not capture the attitudes and drug-using behaviors of school-aged persons who have dropped out of school or have been expelled.)

As a comparison, cigarette use among high school students has continued to decline since the mid to late 1990s while marijuana use remained steady until its recent upswing since the mid-2000s. Rates of past month marijuana use exceeded those of past month cigarette use across all grades: 7.2% vs. 6.1% of 8th graders, 17.6% vs. 11.8% of 10th graders, and 22.6% vs. 18.7% of 12th graders, used marijuana vs. cigarettes, respectively. Research has also indicated an association between early marijuana use and later illicit drug use, as well as later tobacco use and nicotine dependence.

The American Academy of Pediatrics (AAP) suggests that based on the experiences of alcohol and tobacco, "legalization of marijuana would have a negative effect on youth." The AAP predicts that if marijuana were legalized, perceived risk of harm would likely decrease in conjunction with increases in use. ASAM concurs with the AAP that legalization would have the unintended consequences of decreasing the perceived harm associated with marijuana use and thus would be associated with increases in rates of marijuana use. The legalization of marijuana would produce serious public health harms, including increased marijuana use, among youth.

Legalization and Increased Use

The Senate Caucus on International Narcotics Control noted that along with changes in marijuana use rates and corresponding changing attitudes about marijuana use, legal changes have been made at the state level regarding the status of marijuana, stating that "the increasing trend in marijuana production in states with permissive medical marijuana laws cannot be ignored given the considerable danger domestic cultivation poses to changing attitudes among American youth." And yet, when considering alternatives to the federal scheduling of cannabis under the Controlled Substances Act (CSA), the Senate caucus stated, "We believe focusing resources on alternative medicine development through an approved [Food and] Drug Administration (FDA) process, rather than the legalization of marijuana, is the best route to explore."

The College on Problems of Drug Dependence (CPDD), in its public policy statement on drug policy, makes the point that rates of consumption of a drug in a population correlate directly with availability: "The more available a drug of abuse, the more people use it, the more is consumed by the user, and the higher is the number of users who encounter problems caused by heavy use. Therefore, legal controls (including but not necessarily limited to prohibitions) that restrict availability are effective means of reducing consumption, reducing drug-induced problems, and discouraging initial use by children and adolescents."

A 2008 publication from the Marijuana Policy Project (MPP), an organization that seeks to legalize marijuana, suggested that "medical" marijuana laws do not increase teen marijuana use, showing that rates of teen marijuana use in the years of law passage in the mid to late 1990s were higher than those in the mid-2000s but analysis has shown that from 2002 to 2008, rates of marijuana use among adolescents in "medical" marijuana states were higher than youth in states without those laws. Although research is unclear as to why rates of marijuana use were different among youth in these states, it does not follow that making marijuana more accessible at the state level would reduce marijuana use among youth. ASAM has stated that it clearly "opposes any changes in law and regulation that would lead to a sudden significant increase in the availability of any dependence-producing drug (outside of a medically prescribed setting for therapeutic indications)." The availability of marijuana would surely increase under state-based legalization and a substantial marijuana industry would emerge under legalization, as has begun to happen with the legalization of "medical" marijuana.

Many in support of marijuana legalization disregard concerns about the potential increases in the availability of marijuana and/or increases in marijuana use should such laws be passed. The negative health effects of marijuana use often are overlooked or unknown. However, a clear-cut negative health consequence of legalization of marijuana sale and use would be an increase in the number of persons, including youth, in need of treatment services for cannabinoid or marijuana addiction. ASAM, as an organization devoted to the science of addiction medicine, is particularly concerned about this potential rise in population-level addiction rates.

> "*Despite its benefits, decriminalization falls short in many ways—largely because it still lies within the framework of* prohibition."

Marijuana Should Be Fully Legalized, Not Just Decriminalized

Drug Policy Alliance

In the following viewpoint, the Drug Policy Alliance argues that marijuana prohibition has failed, but marijuana decriminalization policies do not go far enough to remedy the problems with prohibition. The alliance contends that decriminalization does not prevent arrests and criminal records, and does nothing to address the harms of the underground—and often violent—marijuana trade. The alliance contends that marijuana ought to be legal, taxed, and regulated in a manner similar to alcohol. The Drug Policy Alliance is a national advocacy leader of drug law reform that is grounded in science, compassion, health, and human rights.

Drug Policy Alliance, "Why Is Marijuana Decriminalization Not Enough?," Drugpolicy .org, January 2015, pp. 1–4. Copyright © 2015 Drug Policy Alliance. All rights reserved. Reproduced with permission.

As you read, consider the following questions:

1. According to the Drug Policy Alliance, in addition to Washington, DC, how many states have enacted various forms of marijuana decriminalization or legalization?

2. According to the viewpoint, New York's decriminalization law has what kind of so-called loophole?

3. The author contends that what country recently became the first country in the world to legalize and regulate the marijuana trade?

Marijuana prohibition has been a costly failure. In 2013, there were 693,482 marijuana arrests in the U.S.—more than 45 percent of all drug arrests. Nearly 88 percent were for simple possession, not sale or manufacture. There are more arrests for marijuana possession every year than for all violent crimes combined. Yet marijuana is the most widely used illegal drug in the U.S. and the world. More than 114 million Americans—more than 43 percent of U.S. residents surveyed—admit to having tried marijuana at least once in their lives, and nearly 20 million to having used it in the past month.

The Rejection of Prohibition

Marijuana arrests also disproportionately affect young people of color. Drug use and drug selling occur at similar rates across racial and ethnic groups. Yet black and Latino individuals are arrested for possessing or selling marijuana at vastly disproportionate rates. In fact, black people were nearly four times more likely to be arrested for possession than white people in 2010.

Prohibition empowers criminal organizations and contributes to violence, crime and corruption on a massive scale—from U.S. street corners to places like Mexico, where more than 100,000 people have been killed since 2006 in the country's drug war.

Eighteen states and Washington, D.C., have enacted various forms of marijuana decriminalization or legalization [while four states have begun to legally regulate marijuana for adults over 21]. Decriminalization is commonly defined as the reduction or elimination of criminal penalties for minor marijuana possession. Many of these states have replaced criminal sanctions with the imposition of civil, fine-only penalties; others have reduced marijuana possession from a felony to a fine-only misdemeanor.

Evidence from states and countries that have reduced penalties not only shows no increase in marijuana or other drug use, but also substantial reductions in misdemeanor arrests where decriminalization has been implemented effectively. In 2011, California reclassified marijuana possession as an infraction (administrative violation) instead of a misdemeanor, leading to "a significant decline in misdemeanor marijuana arrests," which plunged from 54,849 in 2010 to 7,764 in 2011—a decrease of more than 85 percent. Overall misdemeanor drug arrests declined from 129,182 in 2010 to between 75,000 and 81,000 in 2011–2013.

Why Decriminalization Is Not Enough

Despite its benefits, decriminalization falls short in many ways—largely because it still lies within the framework of *prohibition*. Consequently, decriminalization still suffers from the inherent harms of prohibition—namely, an illegal, unregulated market; the unequal application of the laws (regardless of severity of penalty) toward certain groups, especially people of color; unregulated products of unknown potency and quality; and the potential for continued arrests as part of a "net-widening" phenomenon.

Under decriminalization, marijuana possession arrests may continue, or even increase, because police may be more inclined to make arrests if they present less administrative burdens as infractions, civil offenses, or even misdemeanors (without jail), as opposed to felonies. Such a process—often called "net-widening"—occurred in parts of Australia that decriminalized marijuana, where the number of people arrested (but not booked) actually increased. Because many could not afford to pay the fines imposed after an arrest, the result was [according to Peter Reuter] "an increase in the number of individuals being incarcerated for marijuana offenses, albeit now indirectly for their failure to pay a fine."

A misdemeanor conviction, moreover, can seriously hinder an individual's ability to succeed and participate in society by preventing him or her from obtaining employment, housing and student loans. Even an arrest record can be an obstacle to opportunities for otherwise law-abiding individuals.

Additionally, not *all* decriminalization schemes protect *all* people from risk of arrest. Even in many of the states that have reduced penalties, marijuana possession is not fully "decriminalized." Some states have defined simple marijuana possession as only one-half ounce or even less; possession of more than these amounts may still trigger harsh criminal penalties. Some states have only decriminalized a first offense, while subsequent offenses are punished severely. Other states' laws have loopholes, such as New York's, in which personal possession is formally decriminalized, but possession in "public view" remains a crime; as a result, the NYPD [New York City Police Department] still arrested nearly 29,000 people in 2013—87 percent of whom were black or Latino. Marijuana possession arrests under New York City mayor Bill de Blasio in 2014 are on track to equal—or even surpass—the number of arrests under his predecessor, Mayor Michael Bloomberg— and at roughly the same racially disparate rates.

The Harms of Prohibition

Decriminalization will also do nothing to eliminate the lucrative underground market for marijuana, estimated to be worth $40 billion or more in the U.S. This immense market is completely untaxed, a source of revenue that federal and state governments can ill-afford to neglect.

Instead, prohibition ensures that this vast market enriches criminal organizations and produces massive violence, crime and corruption. Virtually all marijuana-related violence is the result of prohibition, which keeps responsible businesses out of the market. Illegal businesses have no legitimate means to settle disputes, so violence inevitably results—as it did during alcohol prohibition.

The effect has been unending bloodshed in countries like Mexico, where at least 100,000 people have been killed in prohibition-related violence since late 2006. Marijuana prohibition is a major cause of this carnage; in fact, one scholar [Reuter] recently argued, "Perhaps the most serious harms [of marijuana] relate to its trafficking and production in Mexico. . . . It has caused great harm to Mexico, as a source of both homicides and corruption."

The federal government has asserted that "[M]arijuana distribution in the United States remains the single largest source of revenue for the Mexican cartels," and is "a cash crop that finances corruption and the carnage of violence year after year." Estimates by the RAND Corporation and the Mexican Institute for Competitiveness project that legalizing marijuana nationally in the U.S. could reduce cartels' drug export revenues by between one-fifth and one-third.

Taxation and Regulation

Legal regulation is not a step into the unknown—we have more than a century of experience in legally regulating thousands of different drugs. Legal regulation means common-sense controls—marijuana wouldn't be treated like Coca-Cola, available to anyone of any age, anywhere, at any time. Under most regulatory proposals, it would be taxed and regulated in a manner similar to alcoholic beverages, with age limits, licensing requirements, quality controls, and other regulatory restrictions. Just as cities, counties and states vary in the way they regulate alcohol, the same could be true for marijuana.

In November of 2012, residents of Colorado and Washington took the historic step of rejecting the failed policy of marijuana prohibition by deciding to permit the legal regulation of marijuana sales, cultivation and distribution for adults 21 and older. Both states have completely eliminated all penalties for personal marijuana possession by adults; Colorado also allows adults to cultivate six marijuana plants. These states determined that simply eliminating criminal penalties for possession was not enough. Both have established sensible regulations for the cultivation, distribution and sale of marijuana to adults.

Alaska, Oregon and Washington, D.C., voted to legalize marijuana in 2014, and legislators and activists in several other states will likely follow suit in the coming years. In Congress, a bipartisan group of legislators has introduced historic legislation to end federal marijuana prohibition. Internationally, Uruguay recently became the first country in the world to legalize and regulate the marijuana trade. Additional legalization proposals are under consideration in several other countries.

Revenue from taxation of marijuana sales could reach up to $8.7 billion per year if taxed like alcohol or tobacco—on top of billions in saved law enforcement resources. The New York City Comptroller's Office [John C. Liu] recently estimated "the total fiscal impact of legalizing marijuana in New York City at roughly $431 million annually." A cost-benefit analysis [by Stephen Pudney, Mark Bryan, and Emilia Del Bono] of regulating marijuana in England and Wales estimated "overall net external benefits in the range £0.5–1.25 billion."

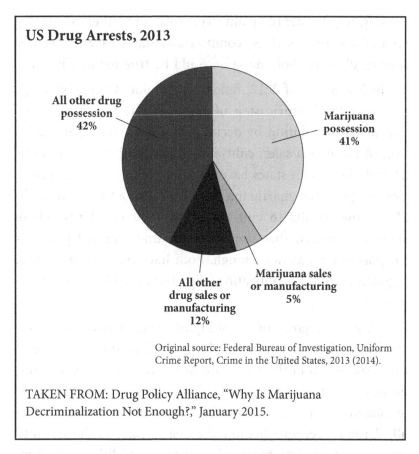

US Drug Arrests, 2013

All other drug
possession
42%

Marijuana
possession
41%

All other
drug sales or
manufacturing
12%

Marijuana sales
or manufacturing
5%

Original source: Federal Bureau of Investigation, Uniform
Crime Report, Crime in the United States, 2013 (2014).

TAKEN FROM: Drug Policy Alliance, "Why Is Marijuana
Decriminalization Not Enough?," January 2015.

A Shift in Opinion

In August of 2013, the Department of Justice (DOJ) announced that it will allow states to legally regulate the production, distribution, and sale of marijuana. The DOJ issued a directive to U.S. attorneys, outlining federal priorities for
enforcing marijuana laws in states that have legalized. While
reserving its right to challenge state laws and enforce federal
marijuana laws under certain circumstances, the directive
states that the federal government will coordinate with states,
rather than seek to interfere, unless states fail to meet certain
federal priorities, such as preventing access by minors, diversion of marijuana, increases in violence or drugged driving, or
damage to public lands.

In its memo, the DOJ openly acknowledged the many benefits of legal regulation:

[S]trong and effective regulatory and enforcement systems to control the cultivation, distribution, sale, and possession of marijuana ... may affirmatively address [federal] priorities by, for example ... prevent[ing] diversion of marijuana outside of the regulated system and to other states, prohibiting access to marijuana by minors, and replacing an illicit marijuana trade that funds criminal enterprises with a tightly regulated market in which revenues are tracked and accounted for.

The administration's new policy is consistent with the will of the people of Colorado and Washington, as well as a substantial majority of American voters, who strongly oppose federal intervention in these states. Indeed, public support for making marijuana legal has shifted dramatically in the last two decades, with recent polls showing greater than majority support nationwide.

| "Legalizing marijuana is not the answer."

Marijuana Should Not Be Legalized

Charles "Cully" Stimson

In the following viewpoint, Charles "Cully" Stimson argues that legalizing marijuana would only worsen the drug situation in the United States. Stimson contends that it is false that marijuana is similar to alcohol, claiming that marijuana has greater harms. Additionally, Stimson says that the purported benefits of legalization put forth by proponents are not supported by research. He concludes that the best way forward is continued prohibition aimed at preventing drug use. Stimson is a senior legal fellow at the Heritage Foundation and manager of the foundation's National Security Law Program in the Davis Institute for International Studies.

As you read, consider the following questions:

1. Stimson contends that unlike alcohol, marijuana is usually consumed to the point of what?

2. What international city does Stimson cite as an example of having a failed experiment in relaxing its policy on marijuana?

Charles "Cully" Stimson, "Why We Shouldn't Legalize Marijuana," Dailycaller.com, July 19, 2012. Copyright © 2012 The Daily Caller. All rights reserved. Reproduced with permission.

3. Stimson claims that the United States ought to have a sound national drug policy like the one under which past US president?

Marijuana is an addictive, gateway drug. It significantly impairs bodily and mental functions, and its use is related to increased violence. These are facts.

Yet proponents of legalizing the drug studiously deny or downplay the well-documented dark side of marijuana trafficking and use. Instead, they promise benefits ranging from reduced crime to additional tax revenue.

Marijuana Is Not Similar to Alcohol

Marijuana advocates have had some success in arguing that marijuana is a "soft" drug, similar to alcohol, and fundamentally different from "hard" drugs like cocaine or heroin. To equate alcohol with marijuana, however, is both uninformed and misleading. Their similarities run only skin deep.

A glass of wine with dinner, for example, has been shown to actually improve health. Not so with marijuana. Though it may have some palliative effects, marijuana has no known general healthful properties.

Instead, clinical studies reveal that long-term, moderate consumption of the drug impairs short-term memory, slows reaction time, increases the risk of heart attack, and can result in birth defects, strokes, and damage to the respiratory system and brain.

Lacking curative or preventive powers, marijuana—unlike alcohol—is usually consumed to the point of intoxication. Prolonged use has a negative effect on cognitive ability that persists beyond the period of intoxication.

What about addiction? Legalization advocates note that alcohol and tobacco are addictive, yet legal. Yes, but marijuana is more likely to cause addiction. One study found that more than 30 percent of adults who used marijuana in the course of a year became dependent on it, exhibiting compulsive behavior and signs of withdrawal.

No Benefits to Society

But think of the benefits to society, pot proponents then argue. Legalizing marijuana would slash drug-related crime, they assert. Yet if and when states legalize marijuana, local demand will increase. Meanwhile, some reputable growers, manufacturers, and retailers will refuse to produce or distribute the drug because of standing federal laws and the tort liability that attend to such a dangerous product. The vacuum will be filled by illegal drug cartels and a black or gray market.

Furthermore, the National Research Council has concluded that the "long-term use of marijuana may alter the nervous system in ways that do promote violence." No place serves as a better example than Amsterdam. Though often touted as a well-functioning city with a relaxed attitude toward drugs, Amsterdam is also one of the most violent cities in Europe. In California, as well, the areas around cannabis clubs have experienced exponential increases in crime rates.

Pot pushers also offer pie-in-the-sky economic arguments on behalf of their cause. Taxes collected from marijuana sales will easily outweigh the social costs of legalization, they say.

In encouraging Californians to vote for the Regulate, Control and Tax Cannabis Act of 2010 [also known as California Proposition 19], the National Organization for the Reform of Marijuana Laws (NORML) predicted a billion-dollar windfall for the state in tax revenues and enforcement savings. A RAND Corporation study subsequently found these projections were riddled with unfounded assumptions. To date, no realistic cost-benefit analysis has been done, yet proponents keep repeating these groundless claims.

Finally, regardless of state law, marijuana remains illegal under federal laws, which states have no authority to allow their citizens to contravene.

The Best Strategy

Legalizing marijuana is not the answer. Rather, sound national drug policy includes international cooperation, research, strengthened law enforcement, treatment, and prevention and education. When President Ronald Reagan adopted a similar strategy, illegal drug use by young adults dropped by more than 50 percent.

Thus, the best option going forward is for states to commit to a comprehensive, unified approach aimed at preventing illegal drug use and reducing the number of drug users.

No state will likely be allowed to legalize marijuana on its own due to negative cross-state spillover effects. Yet even if a state could do so, legalizing marijuana would serve little purpose other than to worsen the drug problem.

> *"Gallup's trend data also makes it clear that legalizing marijuana remains a much easier task in certain places than others."*

Majority Continues to Support Pot Legalization in U.S.

Lydia Saad

In the following viewpoint, Lydia Saad contends that public support for marijuana legalization has steadily increased over the last several decades, reaching the tipping point of a majority in support in the last several years. Saad claims that support for legalization varies by political party and country region. She argues that if support hovers at half, it will be difficult to expand legalization beyond the liberal parts of the country. Saad is senior editor for Gallup, a research-based, global consulting company.

As you read, consider the following questions:

1. According to Saad, in what year did support for marijuana legalization first hit 50 percent?

Lydia Saad, "Majority Continues to Support Pot Legalization in U.S.," Gallup.com, November 6, 2014. Copyright © 2014 Gallup, Inc. All rights reserved. The content is used with permission; however, Gallup retains all rights of republication.

2. The author claims that a solid majority supports marijuana legalization in what two regions of the United States?

3. What percentage of Americans aged eighteen to thirty-four support marijuana legalization, according to Saad?

A slim majority of Americans, 51%, favor legalizing the use of marijuana—similar to the 50% who supported it in 2011 and 2012, but down from a reading of 58% last year.

The new result is based on an Oct. 12–15 Gallup poll, conducted in the run-up to the midterm elections in which various pro-marijuana policy initiatives went before voters in Oregon, Washington, D.C., and Florida, as well as in several cities in Maine, Michigan and elsewhere. Most of those initiatives succeeded, although a proposed constitutional amendment in Florida to legalize medical marijuana failed with 57% of the vote, just shy of the 60% needed.

Gallup's long-term trend on Americans' support for legalizing marijuana shows that in 1969, just 12% of U.S. adults were in favor. But that swelled to 28% by the late 1970s, and 34% by 2003. Since then, support steadily increased to the point that 50% supported it in 2011. Last year was the first time Gallup found a solid majority in favor, at 58%. That poll was conducted amid heavy news coverage of the imminent implementation of Colorado's marijuana legalization law, which may have contributed to what appears to have been a temporary jump in support. This year, support at 51% is still a majority, but closer to where it was in 2011 and 2012.

Conservatives Still Resist Legalization

Gallup's trend data also makes it clear that legalizing marijuana remains a much easier task in certain places than others. Chiefly, in contrast to high levels of support among liberals and solid support among moderates, less than a third of conservative Americans think marijuana should be legal. As a result, such measures are likely to be more viable in relatively liberal locales, including in Oregon and Washington, D.C., where they have already succeeded, than in conservative bastions like Wyoming, Utah or Arkansas.

This pattern is echoed in the results by party ID, with the same implications about the outlook for marijuana legalization being tied to a state's partisan makeup. Currently, 64% of Americans who identify as or lean Democratic side with legalization, compared with 39% of Republicans.

And in accordance with the regional distribution of red and blue states, with most of the blue—heavily Democratic—states clustered on the coasts, and most of the red—Republican-oriented—states concentrated in the middle and Southern regions of the country, Gallup finds a solid majority supporting legalization of marijuana in the East and West, while in 2014, fewer than half support it in the South and Midwest.

Bottom Line

Public support for legalizing the use of marijuana has clearly increased over the past decade. The question now is whether the momentum will continue to build or level off at a bare majority supporting it.

Last year's finding of 58% in favor was recorded as Colorado was preparing to become the first state to implement a law decriminalizing the use of small amounts of marijuana for recreational use. Although the law passed in November 2012, it did not go into effect until January 2014. Americans may have warmed some to proponents' arguments in 2013 in the ongoing discussion around the Colorado law. More recently, Colorado has been in the news over the sale of marijuana-infused edibles—everything from brownies to gummy bears—and the risk they pose to children, possibly sparking public concern. Also, a year ago, proponents in California were poised to launch a ballot initiative for 2014 to le-

Americans' Support for Legalizing the Use of Marijuana—Recent Trend

Do you think the use of marijuana should be made legal?

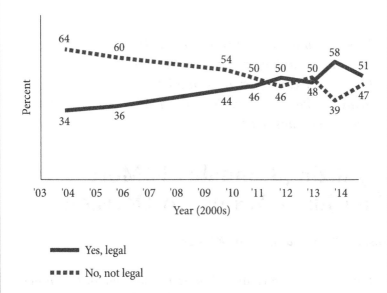

TAKEN FROM: Lydia Saad, "Majority Continues to Support Pot Legalization in U.S.," Gallup, November 6, 2014.

galize marijuana in the Golden State, adding to the sense of momentum for legalization, but later decided to wait until 2016 for fear of losing at the polls, as they did in 2010. The relative lack of attention to new legalization initiatives throughout 2014 may have caused public support to subside.

As long as support hovers around the 50% mark, it will be difficult for proponents to promote legalization beyond the more Democratic and liberal-oriented states. The South and Midwest are likely to remain less hospitable, at least for the time being. But with a super-majority of younger Americans supportive—64% of those aged 18 to 34, contrasted with 41% of those 55 and older—it seems inevitable that this will eventually change.

"It is one thing for a jurisdiction to decide that it no longer supports the prohibition of cannabis; it is another to figure out how to establish and regulate a legal cannabis market."

Legalizing Cannabis Is More than Just a Yes or No Decision

Rosalie Pacula and Beau Kilmer

In the following viewpoint, Rosalie Pacula and Beau Kilmer argue that deciding whether or not to legalize marijuana is merely the first in a long line of decisions that need to be made. Once legalized, rules are necessary to regulate production, distribution, and use; and the authors claim that many lessons can be taken from experience with alcohol and tobacco. They contend that interventions such as keeping the price high and limiting the number of marijuana products available may be beneficial. Pacula and Kilmer are codirectors of the RAND Drug Policy Research Center and professors at the Pardee RAND Graduate School.

As you read, consider the following questions:

1. According to the authors, government agencies have little guidance on how to regulate newly legal markets in what specific ways?

Rosalie Pacula and Beau Kilmer, "Legalising Cannabis Is More than Just a Yes or No Decision," Theconversation.com, May 1, 2014. Copyright © 2014 The Conversation. All rights reserved. Reproduced with permission.

2. The authors contend that both those for and against marijuana legalization share what common public health objectives?

3. What examples do the authors give of new products developed by the alcohol and tobacco industry designed to appeal to young users?

It is one thing for a jurisdiction to decide that it no longer supports the prohibition of cannabis; it is another to figure out how to establish and regulate a legal cannabis market. Uruguay became the first nation to legalise the drug in 2013 but is still working on the full set of rules that will govern production, distribution, and use. Policy makers in Colorado and Washington State, which recently repealed cannabis prohibition, are also grappling with how to do this as other jurisdictions seriously discuss legalisation.

However, many of the details about how to regulate these newly legal markets—determining the number of growers, distributors, and retailers; licensing qualifications; product limitations; quality requirements; and marketing restrictions—are left to government agencies with little guidance on how to do it.

To inform these discussions, we recently published an article which looked at the lessons from the alcohol and tobacco industry. Our goal was not to address whether cannabis legalisation is a good or bad idea but to help policy makers understand the decisions they face and experiences from the regulation of other substances.

The start of any truly honest discussion about how to regulate cannabis markets must start with clear objectives and goals. How these markets are opened can be as important as the decision to legalise cannabis. Knowing which lessons to take away from evidence on alcohol and tobacco regulation very much depends on what these objectives are. Objectives might focus on public health, public safety, personal liberty, restorative justice, maximising revenue, or some combination.

Supporters and Critics Unite

We can start with the premise that many reformers as well as those opposed to legalisation share a common set of public health objectives: to minimise access, availability and use by youths; drugged driving; cannabis dependence and addiction; consumption of products with unwanted contaminants and uncertain potency; and the use of cannabis at the same time as alcohol. The last of these is somewhat controversial, since concurrent use could also reduce alcohol consumption and some of the consequences associated with heavy drinking. But given the research that suggests that concurrent use may also increase traffic crashes and other health harms, it seems appropriate, at least initially, to seek to minimise using them together.

For jurisdictions focused on these five public health objectives there are many lessons to be learned from our experiences with regulating alcohol and tobacco.

There is a large amount of alcohol and tobacco literature demonstrating that consumption and its harms can be reduced by keeping prices artificially high, through taxation for example. After legalisation, we would expect the cost of producing and distributing cannabis to drop as suppliers no longer have to be compensated for their risk and can take advantage of increasing returns to scale. One of the most effective tools for preventing a large drop in retail prices is to create a government-run monopoly. Where this is not possible, regulations can be imposed that create market inefficiencies, such as prohibiting outside production or large greenhouses. Similarly, licenses can be restricted to ensure limited competition with high fees.

Additional production or product requirements can inflate prices, and of course there is the option of excise taxes. Some

Options for Commercial Sale of Marijuana

Commercial sale in a way that fits the alcohol model is not the only alternative to the prohibition of marijuana. Many different options fit the label *legalization*. Policy makers must make choices about what sorts of organizations—for profit, not for profit, or government agencies—would be permitted to produce and sell marijuana, about the prices at which marijuana is sold and how it is taxed, and about what sort of information to provide to consumers, along with a host of regulatory details, such as whether edibles can be sold. Those choices will determine how completely legalization displaces the illicit market, how much problem marijuana use (including use by minors) increases, and how much revenue accrues to governments at specific jurisdictional levels (e.g., state or county).

Jonathan P. Caulkins et al., "Options and Issues Regarding Marijuana Legalization," RAND Corporation, 2015.

of these options—such as requirements to product test and label cannabis products—would have additional benefits like protecting consumers from unwanted contaminants.

There also appear to be advantages, at least initially, to limiting the number and type of products that can be sold. Both the alcohol and tobacco industry have been innovative in developing new products that appeal to young users. Examples include candy and gum cigarettes, alcohol pops, and wine coolers. High-potency cannabis products place users at greater risk of dependence, drugged driving, and other harms if used inappropriately. Restrictions on the type of products allowed could reduce the potential for new products that are particularly attractive to youth, for example cannabis-infused candies and vapouriser pens with flavoured hash oil.

We know from the alcohol and tobacco literature that partial bans on marketing are largely ineffective at limiting use, particularly youth use. While difficult to establish in existing markets, it is conceivable that comprehensive bans on marketing may be possible as a first step away from prohibition.

Other lessons exist as well, such as restricting sales and banning public consumption to reduce youth exposure. It is important to keep in mind that any initial policy is likely to be just a first step; flexibility will need to be built in as knowledge is gained about the real (versus perceived) risks of these products and markets.

Periodical and Internet Sources Bibliography

The following articles have been selected to supplement the diverse views presented in this chapter.

American Civil Liberties Union	"The War on Marijuana in Black and White," June 2013.
William J. Bennett	"Legalizing Drugs Won't Prevent Abuse," CNN, February 15, 2012.
Rebecca Burns	"The Unbearable Whiteness of Legalization," *In These Times*, February 19, 2014.
Tom Dart and Nicky Woolf	"Bid to Legalize Marijuana in Arizona Has Some Advocates Seeing Red," AlterNet, May 7, 2015.
Drug Policy Alliance	"Why Is Marijuana Decriminalization Not Enough?," July 6, 2015.
John Hawkins	"5 Reasons Marijuana Should Remain Illegal," Townhall.com, January 21, 2014.
Patrick Radden Keefe	"Buzzkill," *New Yorker*, November 18, 2013.
Mark Kleiman	"How Not to Make a Hash Out of Cannabis Legalization," *Washington Monthly*, March–May 2014.
Jeffrey Miron	"Why Congress Should Legalize Pot," CNN, November 19, 2014.
Kevin Sabet	"There Are Smarter Ways to Deal with Marijuana than Legalization," *U.S. News & World Report*, October 30, 2012.
Jacob Sullum	"How Is Marijuana Legalization Going? The Price of Pot Peace Looks like a Bargain," *Forbes*, July 10, 2014.
Washington Examiner	"Don't Legalize Marijuana," May 9, 2015.

For Further Discussion

Chapter 1

1. Jamie Chandler and Skylar Young argue that the problem with marijuana prohibition is not the prohibition itself but rather the manner in which it currently focuses on demand. Do you agree with the authors' argument? Why, or why not?

2. Harry Levine argues that marijuana arrests illustrate a pattern of racism in American law enforcement. Heather Mac Donald claims that the arrest rates merely indicate higher crime rates in minority communities. How do you think Levine would respond to Mac Donald's explanation? Explain.

Chapter 2

1. Several authors in this chapter debate the safety of marijuana use in terms of effects on the individual and society. Regarding the legalization of marijuana in a manner comparable to alcohol, how safe does marijuana need to be? Justify your answer drawing upon the viewpoints in this chapter.

2. On what specific issue do Charles D. Stimson and Jeffrey A. Miron make claims that contradict each other? What would one need to know to resolve the issue? Explain.

Chapter 3

1. The Drug Free America Foundation, Inc. (DFAF) argues that marijuana should not be used in plant form as medicine but that its medicinally beneficial components ought to be extracted for medicine after proper research. Name at least two authors of viewpoints in this chapter who you believe would disagree. What do you think their argument against DFAF would be? Explain.

2. Drawing upon the viewpoints of Evan Halper and Debra J. Saunders, what issue that is not solely related to marijuana arises when states pass laws allowing medical use of marijuana? Explain.

Chapter 4

1. Some opponents of prohibition argue that marijuana legalization would result in economic benefits. Name at least one way in which the Office of National Drug Control Policy (ONDCP) would dispute this claim.

2. Rosalie Pacula and Beau Kilmer discuss some of the regulation challenges in implementing legal marijuana. Based on the viewpoints in this chapter and elsewhere in the book, what specific regulation issue do you think would be the most contentious? Explain your reasoning.

Organizations to Contact

The editors have compiled the following list of organizations concerned with the issues debated in this book. The descriptions are derived from materials provided by the organizations. All have publications or information available for interested readers. The list was compiled on the date of publication of the present volume; the information provided here may change. Be aware that many organizations take several weeks or longer to respond to inquiries, so allow as much time as possible.

American Alliance for Medical Cannabis (AAMC)
44500 Tide Avenue, Arch Cape, OR   97102
(503) 436-1882
e-mail: contact@letfreedomgrow.com
website: www.letfreedomgrow.com

The American Alliance for Medical Cannabis (AAMC) is dedicated to bringing patients, caregivers, and volunteers the facts they need to make informed decisions about medical marijuana. AAMC advocates for the rights of medical marijuana patients through education and interaction with government representatives. AAMC's website provides literature on the common medical uses of marijuana.

American Civil Liberties Union (ACLU)
125 Broad Street, 18th Floor, New York, NY   10004
(212) 549-2500
e-mail: aclu@aclu.org
website: www.aclu.org

The American Civil Liberties Union (ACLU) is a national organization that works to defend Americans' civil rights guaranteed by the US Constitution by providing legal defense, research, and education. The ACLU opposes the criminal prohibition of marijuana and the civil liberties violations that result from it. The ACLU Criminal Law Reform Project engages in campaigns and submits briefs in relevant law cases, with literature about these campaigns and text of the briefs available at the ACLU website.

American Society of Addiction Medicine (ASAM)
4601 North Park Avenue, Upper Arcade, Suite 101
Chevy Chase, MD   20815-4520
(301) 656-3920 • fax: (301) 656-3815
e-mail: email@asam.org
website: www.asam.org

The American Society of Addiction Medicine (ASAM) is a professional society representing more than three thousand physicians and associated professionals dedicated to increasing access and improving the quality of addiction treatment. ASAM opposes the legalization of marijuana. The ASAM website has a variety of publications available regarding addiction and the organization's position on drug legalization.

Americans for Safe Access (ASA)
1806 Vernon Street NW, Suite 300, Washington, DC   20009
(202) 857-4272 • fax: (202) 618-6977
e-mail: info@safeaccessnow.org
website: www.safeaccessnow.org

Americans for Safe Access (ASA) is an organization of patients, medical professionals, scientists, and concerned citizens promoting safe and legal access to marijuana for therapeutic use and research. ASA works to overcome political and legal barriers by creating policies that improve access to medical cannabis for patients and researchers through legislation, education, litigation, grassroots actions, advocacy, and services for patients and their caregivers. ASA publishes booklets, available at its website, about the use of cannabis for medical conditions.

Center for Medicinal Cannabis Research (CMCR)
220 Dickinson Street, Suite B, MC8231
San Diego, CA   92103-8231

(619) 543-5024
e-mail: cmcr@ucsd.edu
website: www.cmcr.ucsd.edu

The Center for Medicinal Cannabis Research (CMCR) at the University of California conducts scientific studies intended to ascertain the general medical safety and efficacy of cannabis and cannabis products. CMCR aims to be a resource for health policy planning on the issue of medical marijuana. CMCR provides a list of its published research at its website, with access to select publications.

Drug Free America Foundation, Inc. (DFAF)

5999 Central Avenue, Suite 301, Saint Petersburg, FL 33710
(727) 828-0211 • fax: (727) 828-0212
website: www.dfaf.org

The Drug Free America Foundation, Inc. (DFAF) is a drug prevention and policy organization committed to developing, promoting, and sustaining global strategies, policies, and laws that will reduce illegal drug use, drug addiction, drug-related injury, and death. DFAF opposes efforts that would legalize, decriminalize, or promote illicit drugs, including the legalization of medical or recreational marijuana. DFAF publishes several position statements available at its website, including "Questions and Answers: Marijuana."

Drug Policy Alliance (DPA)

330 Seventh Avenue, 21st Floor, New York, NY 10001
(212) 613-8020 • fax: (212) 613-8021
e-mail: nyc@drugpolicy.org
website: www.drugpolicy.org

The Drug Policy Alliance (DPA) supports and publicizes alternatives to current US policies on illegal drugs, including marijuana. DPA has worked on initiatives in several states to make medical marijuana legally available to ill patients. DPA publishes many research briefs and fact sheets, such as "A Comparison of the World's First Three Jurisdictions to Legally Regulate Marijuana: Colorado, Washington, and Uruguay," which are available at its website.

Marijuana Policy Project (MPP)

PO Box 77492, Capitol Hill, Washington, DC   20013
(202) 462-5747
e-mail: info@mpp.org
website: www.mpp.org

The Marijuana Policy Project (MPP) works to further public policies that allow for responsible medical and nonmedical use of marijuana and that minimize the harms associated with marijuana consumption and the laws that manage its use. MPP works to increase public support for marijuana regulation and lobbies for marijuana policy reform at the state and federal levels. MPP works to increase public awareness through speaking engagements, educational seminars, the mass media, and briefing papers.

National Institute on Drug Abuse (NIDA)

6001 Executive Boulevard, Room 5213, MSC 9561
Bethesda, MD   20892-9561
(301) 443-1124
e-mail: information@nida.nih.gov
website: www.nida.nih.gov

The National Institute on Drug Abuse (NIDA) is part of the National Institutes of Health, a component of the US Department of Health and Human Services, with the mission of using science to address drug abuse and addiction. NIDA supports and conducts research on drug abuse to improve addiction prevention, treatment, and policy efforts. It publishes the bimonthly *NIDA Notes* newsletter, periodic fact sheets, and a catalog of research reports and public education materials on both the medical and recreational use of marijuana.

National Organization for the Reform of Marijuana Laws (NORML)

1100 H Street NW, Suite 830, Washington, DC 20005
(202) 483-5500 • fax: (202) 483-0057
e-mail: norml@norml.org
website: www.norml.org

The National Organization for the Reform of Marijuana Laws (NORML) aims to move public opinion to achieve the repeal of marijuana prohibition so that the responsible use of cannabis by adults is no longer subject to penalty. NORML lobbies state and federal legislators in support of reform legislation, including the end of marijuana prohibition for both medical and personal use. NORML has numerous research and position papers available at its website, including "Marijuana: A Primer."

Office of National Drug Control Policy (ONDCP)

Drug Policy Information Clearinghouse, PO Box 6000
Rockville, MD 20849-6000
(800) 666-3332 • fax: (301) 519-5212
e-mail: ondcp@ncjrs.org
website: www.whitehousedrugpolicy.gov

The Office of National Drug Control Policy (ONDCP), a component of the Executive Office of the President, establishes policies, priorities, and objectives for the nation's drug control program. ONDCP works to reduce illicit drug use, manufacturing, and trafficking; drug-related crime and violence; and drug-related health consequences. ONDCP's website has numerous publications related to its mission, including "State Laws Related to Marijuana."

Partnership for Drug-Free Kids

352 Park Avenue South, 9th Floor, New York, NY 10010
(212) 922-1560 • fax: (212) 922-1570
e-mail: webmail@drugfree.org
website: www.drugfree.org

The Partnership for Drug-Free Kids is a nonprofit organization that works to help parents prevent, intervene in, or find treatment for drug and alcohol use by their children. It offers information, tools, and opportunities to connect with other parents and caregivers who may have a child struggling with addiction. Its website features interactive tools that translate the latest science and research on teen behavior, addiction, and treatment into tips and tools for parents.

Bibliography of Books

Bruce Barcott   *Weed the People: The Future of Legal
                        Marijuana in America.* New York:
                        Time Books, 2015.

William J.   *Going to Pot: Why the Rush to
Bennett and   Legalize Marijuana Is Harming
Robert A. White   America.* New York: Center Street,
                        2015.

Greg Campbell   *Pot, Inc.: Inside Medical Marijuana,
                        America's Most Outlaw Industry.* New
                        York: Sterling, 2012.

Jonathan P.   *Marijuana Legalization: What
Caulkins, Angela   Everyone Needs to Know.* New York:
Hawken, Beau   Oxford University Press, 2012.
Kilmer, and Mark
A.R. Kleiman

Steve DeAngelo   *The Cannabis Manifesto: A New
                        Paradigm for Wellness.* Berkeley, CA:
                        North Atlantic Books, 2015.

Vanda   *Shooting Up: Counterinsurgency and
Felbab-Brown   the War on Drugs.* Washington, DC:
                        Brookings Institution Press, 2010.

Steve Fox, Paul   *Marijuana Is Safer: So Why Are We
Armentano, and   Driving People to Drink?* White River
Mason Tvert   Junction, VT: Chelsea Green
                        Publishing, 2013.

Margaret J.   *Legalizing Drugs: Crime Stopper or
Goldstein   Social Risk?* Minneapolis, MN:
                        Twenty-First Century Books, 2010.

Erich Goode   *Drugs in American Society.* 9th ed.
                       New York: McGraw-Hill, 2014.

James P. Gray   *Why Our Drug Laws Have Failed and
                       What We Can Do About It: A Judicial
                       Indictment of the War on Drugs.* 2nd
                       ed. Philadelphia, PA: Temple
                       University Press, 2012.

Kevin P. Hill   *Marijuana: The Unbiased Truth About
                       the World's Most Popular Weed.*
                       Center City, MN: Hazelden, 2015.

Michael D.   *Drugs in Society: Causes, Concepts,
Lyman   and Control.* 7th ed. New York:
                       Routledge, 2013.

Alyson Martin   *A New Leaf: The End of Cannabis
and Nushin   Prohibition.* New York: New Press,
Rashidian   2014.

Trish Regan   *Joint Ventures: Inside America's Almost
                       Legal Marijuana Industry.* Hoboken,
                       NJ: John Wiley & Sons, 2011.

Michael J.   *Blowing Smoke: Rethinking the War
Reznicek   on Drugs Without Prohibition and
                       Rehab.* Lanham, MD: Rowman &
                       Littlefield Publishers, 2012.

Roger Roffman   *Marijuana Nation: One Man's
                       Chronicle of America Getting High:
                       From Vietnam to Legalization.* New
                       York: Pegasus Books, 2014.

Robin Room,   *Cannabis Policy: Moving Beyond*
Benedikt Fischer, *Stalemate.* New York: Oxford
Wayne Hall,   University Press, 2010.
Simon Lenton,
and Peter Reuter

Kevin A. Sabet   *Reefer Sanity: Seven Great Myths*
                   About Marijuana. New York: Beaufort
                   Books, 2013.

Nicholas Schou   *The Weed Runners: Travels with the*
                   Outlaw Capitalists of America's
                   Medical Marijuana Trade. Chicago,
                   IL: Chicago Review Press, 2013.

Katherine Tate,   *Something's in the Air: Race, Crime,*
James Lance   *and the Legalization of Marijuana.*
Taylor, and Mark   New York: Routledge, 2014.
Q. Sawyer, eds.

Jon Walker   *After Legalization: Understanding the*
                   Future of Marijuana Policy.
                   Washington, DC: FDL Writers
                   Foundation, 2014.

Samuel Walker   *Sense and Nonsense About Crime,*
                   Drugs, and Communities. 8th ed.
                   Stamford, CT: Cengage Learning,
                   2015.

Index

A

Accidents
    and injuries, drug and alcohol
      use, 93, 112, 170
    vehicles, drug and alcohol use,
      43, 88–89, 184–185, 208
Addiction, 89
    alcohol, 106, 108–109
    causes, 33–35, 39, 91–92
    drug treatment, decriminaliza-
      tion policy, 24–28, 37–38
    drugs, potential, 18, 22, 32,
      34, 164
    marijuana addictiveness, 43,
      89–91, 109, 199–200
    marijuana dangers and con-
      siderations, 16, 83, 106, 108–
      109, 178, 188–189, 208
Addictive Behavior (journal), 111
Adolescents. *See* Ages of drug us-
    ers; Children
Affordable Care Act (2010), 43
African Americans
    opinions on legalization, 15
    possession arrests, high-crime
      areas, 57, 59, 62–64
    possession arrests, injustice,
      48, 49, 50, 54, 59, 191
    prison populations, 45
Age, and opinions on legalization,
    14, 160, 205
Ages of drug users
    and addiction risks, 89–90
    and mental development
      risks, 89–91
    possession arrests, 48

protection of children, 33, 38,
    115, 188, 204, 208, 209–210
regulated systems of legaliza-
    tion, 71, 72–73, 76–77, 167,
    185–186, 187, 194–195
teen usage and legalization,
    28–29, 178, 187, 188
teen usage and perceived risk
    of harm, 185*t*, 186, 187
teen/young adult usage and
    arrests, 48, 49
treatment tracking, 24–25
Aggression
    alcohol, 106, 111–112, 118
    marijuana, 111, 121, 200
    See also Violence
Agriculture regulation, 32
Alaska, 71, 135, 167, 195
Alcohol
    addiction, 106, 108–109
    aggression and violence and,
      111–112, 118
    combination with marijuana,
      89, 208
    health- and safety-related
      costs, 107, 109, 112, 117–
      118, 172, 175, 183–184
    health harms, 106–112, 113,
      115–116, 117–119
    marijuana is not safer than,
      198, 199–200
    marijuana is safer than, 106–
      112
    marijuana regulation com-
      pared, 30, 71, 76, 78, 80, 83,
      84, 183–184, 185–186, 190,
      194–195, 207–210

marijuana cultivation, 68
proactive policing effects, 64
Female prison inmates, 69
Fingerprint records, 55
Fire hazards, 150, 176–177
Flake, Jeff, 163
Florida, 203
Food and Drug Administration
(FDA)
approved drugs, 99, 141–142
non-approval of medical
marijuana, 137–138, 152,
153, 173
official approval process, 145,
172–173, 187
study of marijuana, 153
Foreign relations, international
drug markets, 33, 194
Forfeiture laws, 69
Forms of marijuana, 86, 98
Foundation for a Drug-Free
World, 44

G

Galston, William A., 14
Gangs and gang violence
drug-related, 38, 39, 73–74
growing marijuana, 36, 37,
177
See also Drug cartels
Gateway drug argument
described, 85, 91–92
reason for not supporting
legalization, 16, 43, 123–124,
199
Gender, and opinions on legalization, 14–15
General regulation of legal marijuana, 31–32, 69, 71, 72–73, 192

practical details, 122–123,
206–210
state jurisdiction, 196–197
See also Taxation
Generation X (1965-1980), 14
Generations' opinions on legalization, 14, 160, 205
Gerber, Jill, 163
Gillibrand, Kirsten, 162
Giuliani, Rudolph, 64–65
Glaucoma, 99, 101
Grassley, Chuck, 163
Gray markets, 123, 180, 200
Grisanti, Mark, 60
Growing marijuana
criminal sanctions, 68–69,
147, 148
decriminalization and regulation, 31, 37, 71, 132, 148,
149, 195
environmental harms, 176–
177
history, 95, 96–97, 98–99
odors, 122
patients growing medical
marijuana, 132, 146–151
theft and related crime, 122,
123, 150, 177
Gupta, Sanjay, 162
GW Pharmaceuticals, 142, 144–
145

H

Halper, Evan, 156–160
Hansen, Benjamin, 28
Hari, Johann, 33, 35
Harris, Andy, 158
Hawaii, 70, 135